FM

DANCING AT YOUR DESK

A METAPHYSICAL GUIDE TO JOB HAPPINESS

The *Continuum Series* of Books
from Frederick Malowany Publishing

BrilliantDay
7 Quick Solutions to Turn Your Day Around

BrilliantWork
7 Steps to Corporate Mastery

BrilliantLove
10 Steps to a Brilliant Relationship

All FM books are also available through
BrilliantWork™ at **www.brilliantwork.com**
or by phone: 303-939-8574.

Retail / Group discounts available.

BRILLIANTWORK

Putting personal and business power to work...brilliantly.

"The 7 Secret Steps to Finding Work You Love"

DANCING AT YOUR DESK

A METAPHYSICAL GUIDE TO JOB HAPPINESS

BY SUE FREDERICK

Founder of BrilliantWork

FREDERICK **FM** MALOWANY

This edition first published in 2004 by Frederick Malowany Publishing.

10 9 8 7 6 5 4 3 2 1

ISBN# 0-9762393-0-2

Printed in USA

Frederick Malowany Publishing
Post Office Box 17343
Boulder, Colorado 80308

Telephone 303-939-8574

Other books offered in the **Continuum Series**:

Brilliant**Love** *10 Steps to a Brilliant Relationship*

Brilliant**Work** *7 Steps to Corporate Mastery*

Brilliant**Parent** *7 Steps to Brilliant Parenting*

Dancing at Your Desk *7 Secret Steps to Finding Work You Love*
(A Metaphysical Guide to Job Happiness)

All FM books are also available through BrilliantWork™ at
www.brilliantwork.com

PRAISE FOR *Dancing At Your Desk*

"This is life-changing work. It goes way beyond just finding a better job."

Elizabeth Mueller
Raleigh, North Carolina

"My BrilliantWork sessions went way beyond my expectations. The combination of homework, open-ended questions, insights, and visualizations was very powerful. It literally transformed my life."

Dick Augsburger
Chicago, Illinois

"My life has flip-flopped into this beautiful existence – from hell to heaven."

Tonja van Helden
Boulder, Colorado

"What a happy place this planet would be if everyone did this work."

Katherine Bergin, *ChiRunning*
San Rafael, California

"I appreciate this work so very much! I couldn't afford any longer to give my dreams away!"

Victoria Riis
Boulder, Colorado

"Thank you for sharing your brilliant work with our community at Naropa. It is a blessing!"

Charlotte Rotterdam
Director of Programming
Naropa University
Boulder, Colorado

This book is dedicated to

Paul Frederick *and* Crissie Cagle

who both died in their 30s

still searching for work they would love.

TABLE OF CONTENTS

The 7 Secret Steps to Finding Your BrilliantWork

Wake Up

Realize how you've been affecting the events in your life. Learn about your energy continuum and how to use it to find your true work – instead of what you "should" do for a living.

Dream

Your dreams are your keys to happiness; What do you REALLY want?

Search

Find your values, passions, and talents – your NATURAL gifts.

Use Your Energy

to move through pain and fear: Your high-end energy opens doors, sets loose your dream, and guides you to work you love.

See It

Always script the future you want before taking action.

Take Action

Research, network, and interview only while operating from the high-end of your continuum.

Change It

Use the energy of change to move you forward.

"What you believe is what you get."

Sue Frederick

INTRODUCTION

Why a Metaphysical Guide?

    Shortly after discovering these secret principles which I share in **Dancing At Your Desk**, I put them to the test. I was invited to interview for a high-paying job as director of a career counseling center at a Denver College. At the time, I was $90,000 in debt (plus my home mortgage debt) and one inch from bankruptcy that would have cost me and my nine-year-old daughter our home. Clearly, I needed the job. Since I had made a major inner transformation due to the secrets I share in this book, I drove to the interview without a worry in the world. My windows were rolled down, blowing my hair in every direction as I sang at the top of my lungs to my favorite opera score – *La Boheme*.

    I arrived too early for the interview and happily gave the receptionist my name. I sat in the waiting room feeling absolute joy and complete confidence that I would soon be taking my daughter to London to see the Globe Theater (our dream) as I reaped the benefits of my new financial prosperity. I didn't care if I got this job or not. I knew that all would be fabulous in my life, no matter what happened today. As I sat in the waiting room, feeling so much joy it felt like it was pouring from my skin, people who worked for the university began coming out of their respective offices, introducing themselves to me, telling me their stories and exchanging business cards with me. It seemed everyone who worked within a 500 foot range of where I sat suddenly needed to meet me. Several times people from admissions and other departments said to me, "If things don't work out for you in the career services department, please call me. We're always looking for people like you."

I should mention that I'm 51 years old and long past the point where I attract people to me because of my youthful (or otherwise) beauty. It was something else that was attracting them to me – (something that I'll teach you in this book). Soon, 14 other job applicants arrived (most of them looking extremely somber and serious), and we found ourselves facing each other in a very small waiting room as we discovered that we were all applying for the same position and would be interviewed in a group at the same time. The tension in the room was tangible.

I looked down at my black pantsuit and realized that it was covered in cat hair. I had meant to "roll" the hair off when I got out of the car. I pulled the lint roller out of my briefcase and stood up boldly in the center of our little group and began rolling the cat hair off of my suit with huge sweeping movements. Some people chuckled. Most looked horrified.

"Would anyone like to borrow this roller?" I asked loudly. A few people murmured "no thanks" and most of the others ignored me as if I had the plague. The woman sitting next to me giggled and began chatting with me. Soon she was my new best friend and looking very relaxed. After a long wait during which the two hiring managers walked past us several times observing how we were interacting with each other (most people were staring somberly into space), they invited us into a small conference room. We sat down around a long conference table and the managers took either end of the table. For an hour and a half, they asked open-ended questions which everyone in the group had to answer individually. These started with, "In one minute or less, tell us about yourself and why you want this job," to "Your biggest pet peeve is..."

I don't remember what I said, but it came easily and fluidly to me, and I made everyone laugh. I simply didn't care if I said the right thing or not. I simply didn't feel a need to impress anyone. And I was having a great time...even giggling to myself throughout the entire process. I kept my heart feeling happy and content – no matter what.

When I returned home, there were two job offers on my answering machine from different departments at that university – including the career services department. I kept feeling my joy and confidence as I imagined working with all of those folks to create several different opportunities to work with them in the perfect format, bringing in the perfect amount of money. Within two weeks, we had created a consulting job for me that included teaching career workshops and teaching a class called **Finding Work you Love**. These activities were exactly what I loved doing, and what I'm uniquely talented at, and together they brought me a nice income. It was so easy, I was laughing through the entire process. **From that moment on, I knew that I had indeed stumbled on the absolutely effective secrets of finding and creating work you love. Now I'm going to share them with you.**

It's all physics, my dear...
and that is our secret.

But we'll discuss more about that later. Here's another example…

Gregg's Story

Gregg was a laid-off tech worker from a large corporation when he came to me for career counseling. "I should search for another high-tech job in order to support my family," he explained. However, his heart just wasn't in it. He longed for a different kind of career path – one that followed his passions and dreams. Yet he had no clarity about what that path was. He made a list of five "new directions" to pursue. These included becoming a chef, a realtor, and opening a retail business.

I explained to Gregg that the answer to his search was already inside of him. "It's just a matter of finding out what you're really longing for," I explained.

During our first session, I took him through the BrilliantWork guided visualization process – imagining a day in the life of several different careers. After the exercise, he said he couldn't even swallow when he imagined himself going back to work at a tech job. He felt like he couldn't breathe. But as he imagined a day in the life of being a chef, his body felt alive, renewed, eager to do this work.

Then I played my "two million dollar game" with Gregg. I told him I was putting $2 million in his bank account so that he had no money concerns – yet he still had to work. "What career would you choose if you already had all the money you wanted yet you still had to work?" I asked him.

Immediately he answered, "I'd be a chef. I love working with food."

Step by step, I taught him to hold on to that high-end energy when he imagined his new career as chef, and to keep that energy guiding him whenever he called or wrote or interviewed anyone about this new career. Soon he could create that high-end feeling at will, and it became his ally in creating his new life.

Together, we created a plan that included getting a part-time job to bring in income while he attended cooking school. Six months later, Gregg had a new and much richer life. By giving voice to his dreams and using the energy that he felt when he pictured this career to attract opportunities, he was able to create a new life for himself and his family.

As a career counselor, I spent years helping people identify their joyful work (what I call BrilliantWork). Most of my clients then went on to transform their lives. But some didn't make the transformation and remained stuck. Finally I figured out why.

In this book, I will teach you first to identify your BrilliantWork, and then how to use the secret ingredient, or the metaphysical principle, that then attracts this joyful work to you.

This recipe for attracting it into your life takes all the head-banging, drudgery, and tediousness out of changing careers. It creates immediate results. What I will share with you in this book is simple and more effective than anything you could ever imagine. And that's why it goes beyond all the great career books you've ever read. It works – like magic.

What is BrilliantWork?

"Just get a job, any job."

You've probably been told, at some point in your life, to just get a job. My advice is to ignore that advice completely. Throw it out the window. It's time to launch your working life in a way that will reap happiness, meaning, joy and fulfillment, as well as financial reward. That doesn't mean doing what everyone says you "should" do.

The first step is to understand what "work" is really about. Making money is not the sole purpose of work in today's culture. Money is a result and a benefit that comes from finding your joyful work, which is what I call your BrilliantWork.

Family and friends may have told you that we only work to make money. Ask yourself: Will money alone bring me happiness? It won't. I promise. Think of it this way: You spend more than 85% of your waking hours at a job. Imagine spending most of your waking hours at a job that is meaningless to you, or that doesn't utilize your innate talents and gifts, and leaves you feeling exhausted and depressed. Do you think you will feel fulfilled and content doing this type of work day-after-day?

What you're really searching for is joy and happiness.
You're spending most of your waking hours at work – therefore you must find that joy and happiness at work as well as in your personal life. The first step is identifying what you truly want in your life and focusing on that. This guides you to your passions. And your passions are the key!

Your BrilliantWork is much bigger than something you "should" do. It's your unique work path that utilizes your unique gifts and dreams. It brings you success and fulfillment because it's driven by your passions. It's your joyful work – the work that transforms you and brings your light to the world.

The choice is yours. Will you live with a limited viewpoint of what you're capable of and how wonderful your life can be? Or will you take a chance and believe that greater job happiness and success can be yours?

The work that you do now to find the right career path will reward you with joy, a sense of purpose, and financial success. By the way, the most successful people in the world, the millionaires, are the ones who feel most passionate about their work. They not only love their work, they think it's great fun! They adore it! They don't go to work with a sense of drudgery or duty. They go to work driven by a passion from the heart. From Oprah to Ralph Lauren to Steven Spielberg, our culture is filled with examples of successful people who have followed their passions to create joyful work – which led them to their fortunes. Your task is to find your passion and use that high-energy feeling as a guide to your joyful work. In other words, identify this wonderful new path and feel how exhilarating your life will be when you love your work. Then let that energy guide you, and doors will open.

Recognize that your energy is interacting with every person and circumstance in your life to make it either better or worse. Learn to master your energy and you have the power to make your dreams come true.

First you need to know what you really want – not just what you should want. Making a decision to be true to your unique self and your unique dreams opens many doors. Making a decision based upon fear (which means choosing what you "should" do rather than what you long to do) creates a pattern for making fear-based decisions. Soon you've built a life based on fear rather than joy, and limited happiness in very small doses will be yours. When you use high-end energy and passion to guide you, you create a pattern for living courageously. Soon it becomes a way of life.

I used to be a mountaineering/survival instructor for Colorado Outward Bound School. I led groups of people through the Colorado Rockies and taught them to rock climb, summit mountains, and most of all, to find their courage. When a student would try something they were terrified of, such as rock climbing, and see that they could live through it and possibly enjoy it, they felt more confident to try something else they were afraid of. At the end of these three-week survival courses, people felt empowered and eager to live with more courage and determination. Each courageous step built upon a previous one.

In this book, I teach you how to make career choices based on joy, passion, intention and optimism (your high-end energy) rather than fear, anxiety, lack or depression (your negative energy). I will continually ask you, "What do you really want?" By answering honestly, you will build a life based on courage and positive energy rather than fear and negativity.

Your BrilliantWork is your joyful work.

The nature of our work defines us, and not the other way around. Social psychologists have long studied the effect that certain job "roles" have on human personalities. For example, white-collar executives who find themselves working as prison guards eventually act and think like prison guards. How does your work define you?

"It's what you do that makes your soul, and not the other way around."

Barbara Kingsolver, Animal Dreams

In other words, our self esteem, how we define ourselves, is deeply connected to the work we do in the world. Ask yourself what traits are valued at a job. Are these the traits you want to nurture in yourself? Is this how you want to interact with the world? When you meet someone new, what is the first question they ask you? "What do you do for a living?" How does your answer feel to you? Does it make you happy?

As the poet *David Whyte* says:

"Work is where the self meets the world."

When I discuss "BrilliantWork," I mean work that brings your unique gifts to the world, and makes you feel good while you're doing it. For example, one of my workshop attendees was working unhappily as a health journalist. Her work was meaningful to her, however, she had a gift for creativity, personal style, fashion and design. These talents were not valued in her career, yet they were essential to her innate nature. She was not enjoying her work or her life.

In my workshop, she made plans to open a Vintage-clothing store where her unique gifts and abilities could be used everyday. Bringing her innate creativity and style to the world was her BrilliantWork. She felt happy and inspired when she imagined outfitting women in beautiful clothing. This new direction used her unique gifts and made her feel joyful. What is your BrilliantWork?

Do you know the story of Ralph Lauren who built an empire from his dream? You might not think that a fashion designer is serving the world in a meaningful way. But listen to this story: Ralph Lauren grew up very poor in New York City, but he always had a vision, an innate passion for style. His heroes were Jimmy Stewart and Cary Grant because of their unique, classy elegance.

As a child, Lauren was forced to wear torn up hand-me-down clothing to school – in spite of his innate passion for style and grace. He felt shame because of the way he looked, and the clothes he wore. He dreamed of looking stylish and graceful like Cary Grant. When he was a teenager, he found scraps of silk and designed elegant men's ties. He sold them to local stores and soon had clients such as Saks Fifth Avenue. He followed his vision to create a unique line of clothing. His passion fueled his success. Today he feels a deep sense of satisfaction from his work because he's helping people dress with style and elegance; helping them feel good about themselves. He loves the creativity in his work. His business is fun and meaningful to him. In his unique way, Ralph Lauren is serving the world with his talents, passions and gifts. It is his BrilliantWork.

As the poet *Rabindranath Tagore* wrote:

I slept and dreamt that life was joy.

I awoke and saw that life was service.

I acted and behold, service was joy.

Six Promises to Make to Yourself

1. I **will** find work I love.

2. The work I love **will** create financial abundance.

3. I **will** feel happiness and peace every day – no matter my circumstances.

4. I **will** direct my energies towards the future I dream of, and I **will** ignore current circumstances that make me unhappy.

5. I will not give up when I am afraid.

6. I will not give up when I am tired.

Chapter One

WAKE UP!

Realize how you've been affecting the events in your life.

I'm going to teach you the metaphysical principles that will guarantee you career happiness and financial abundance to go with it. However, the first step is identifying what you DO want in your life. That happens when you begin to understand how your mind affects your life – both positively and negatively.

First, I'm going to tell you my story – about the moment that transformed my life. It happened in my acupuncturist's office one morning and only took 15 minutes. Here's how it went:

I awoke on a November morning, to hear a voice inside my head saying, "Welcome back to the nightmare." Immediately, I went back into my terror of bankruptcy, losing my home, and ruining my daughter's life. I could feel this terror in my body, in my stomach, and it was making me physically ill. As a single mom of a nine-year-old daughter, I had launched a business while living on a second mortgage (which was now gone), and I had massive credit card debt. The bill collectors called everyday.

I felt so physically ill that I went to see my acupuncturist that morning after I took my daughter to school. While he was treating me, I talked about my fear of ruining my daughter's life, of losing our home, and I cried and cried. He listened. He waited. When I had gone on long enough about my looming disasters, he spoke calmly and clearly.

"Sue, the universe operates according to the law of physics. It doesn't care a hoot about all of your hard work, your good intentions or your wonderful daughter. It simply feels your vibrations and sends you back more of the same. Every moment that you spend in this state of fear, you are attracting exactly what you fear into your life. It's simply physics."

He asked me what my life would look like if he suddenly gave me $200,000. I took a huge sigh of relief and told him how I would pay off all of my debts, and Sarah I would take a trip to London to see the Globe Theater because she loves Shakespeare. As I began describing to him in detail what that would be like, I felt lighter and happier until I was giggling as I talked about it.

"Do you see how quickly you shifted your feelings and now feel joy instead of fear, even though nothing in your circumstances has really changed?" he asked. "Hold onto that new feeling as if you had that new life, and you will begin attracting it."

Then he left the room. As I lay on the treatment table with acupuncture needles stuck in various places, I felt new, healthy energy surging through my body. I had always experienced this elevated energy through acupuncture treatment. I had also experienced it through various forms of meditation, chanting and prayer at various times in my life. But for the first time, I realized that I could shift my energy in a second, by shifting my feelings from fear to joy. And I suddenly realized how easy and how brilliant it was.

Ten minutes later when he reappeared back into the treatment room, we discussed a few more details of his ideas; we discussed how these principles have been explained in different ways in various traditions from *Course in Miracles* to Buddhism and Hinduism. As a student of spirituality, I had prayed and meditated everyday for more than 30 years. But the missing link for me had been realizing that my feelings were creating my vibrations, and that I could change my feelings in an instant – no matter my circumstances. And suddenly, in one moment, I gained control of my life for the first time.

From that moment on, I saw my life in a completely different way. I realized that my work as a career counselor had sometimes transformed people's lives because I had successfully given those clients a vision of their ideal work/life to hold onto – while they went about doing all the "right" career actions. Yet other clients hadn't been able to feel what this new career would feel like, and thus hadn't been able to transform their lives. Ultimately, they hadn't been able to raise their energy vibrations to attract positive opportunities.

AND I began to see which techniques I had been using successfully with clients to get them to FEEL their new careers, and use their energy as a positive force for change. My practice then changed completely. My business took off, my clients had miraculous results from my work, and my bank account grew substantially. My life has never been the same.

Now I'm going to share all of this with you. And you will, by the time you have completed this book, have identified and created your joyful work – your Brilliant Work. **This unique combination of career exercises that uncover your hidden dreams, desires and talents – coupled with these simple metaphysical concepts is guaranteed to work for you! It's the law of physics!**

How does this work?

All of us have a million reasons to feel bad at any given moment during our day. Circumstances change for the better and for the worse in a constant flow of events. We react to those circumstances as we've been taught to by our families, teachers, and friends. We believe we have little choice in how we react. And even if we did react in a different way, what would it matter? This is truly the "human condition."

Quantum physicists and all the great spiritual teachers have aligned themselves behind one idea – everything is energy. Everything you see, sit on, feel – the sun on your face, children's laughter, a good run, prayer, a great kiss – is all source energy: that which everything and every-one came from.

You are composed of this same energy – and its frequency can be raised or lowered according to your thoughts, feelings and beliefs. The frequency you send out at any given time attracts like frequencies. Like attracts like.

For example, when I'm feeling joy and gratitude, my vibration puts me on a plane where I can connect with and attract other elements that vibrate on the higher plane. Thus, I can bring wonderful things into my life when I'm feeling good. (Haven't you noticed this is true? When you're having a great day, wonderful things happen to you all day long. When you're having a bad day, things seem to get worse and worse, don't they?)

Here's the surprise: These ups and downs are because of YOUR energy – not because of external forces working on you. Each of us has an energy continuum – negative at the bottom, positive at the top. Positive energy includes our brilliance, goodness, divinity, inspiration, love, passion, optimism, happiness and joy (our connectedness).

Negative energy includes our anger, depression, sadness, guilt, pessimism, meanness, sense of lack, drudgery and separateness – not only from others, but from our source energy.

Everyday we bounce up and down on this continuum depending on our circumstances. We say, if only my circumstances would change I could be happy. The ultimate irony is that if we get happy, our circumstances will change to meet us.

Moving up your energy continuum (in spite of circumstances) by changing your energy to a higher frequency and opening up to source energy connects you to your inspiration, spirituality and goodness. It changes your life immediately!

See your energy continuum as a fuel gauge. When your fuel tank in your car nears empty, you worry about running out of gas and being stranded – which is separateness and stagnation. When it's full, you're confident and able to explore. You have unlimited energy and ideas – which is connectedness, inspiration and productivity.

Consider that you are in control of what level you vibrate on, thus you are in control of what happens to you in any given day.

And the simple, even silly revelation here is that your emotions determine what level you're vibrating on. So when you feel love and joy, you're at the highest level attracting the most wonderful things into your life. When you're feeling despair, you attract more of the same.

No matter how positive your energy is, you will still have challenging events happen to you. We sign up for those (karmas) in order to learn and grow. However, your reaction to those events determines their outcome. Your energy level determines whether you react well or poorly to a crisis. A good life requires good energy. It's that simple.

You might be thinking, well it just makes me feel worse to believe I'm responsible for my own unhappiness. Think of it this way: It's simply physics. The universe operates on the same physical laws of physics that control gravity and make our refrigerator magnets stick to the refrigerator door. The universe doesn't hear words or care about all the great things you're doing to make your life better. It only feels your vibrations (which come from your feelings), and then answers your vibratory call with more of the same. (You can ask for divine guidance and get help changing your energy).

In this book, I will teach you many ways to fill your energy tank so that when you search for work you love, you'll be using your high–octane energy to fuel your efforts. It's simply the law of physics that this high–end energy will create great results in your life.

Now, speaking of physics...here are some things to think about as you go on this journey with me. In his brilliant book, *The Self-Aware*

Universe, physicist Amit Goswami, Ph.D., contends that we must give up our precious assumption that there is an objective reality out there independent of consciousness. He explains that the universe is "self-aware"and that it is consciousness itself that creates the physical world. He comes to this conclusion by way of quantum physics.

To put it in Goswami's words: **"Quantum physics presents a new and exciting worldview that challenges old concepts, such as deterministic trajectories of motion and causal continuity. If initial conditions do not forever determine an object's motion, if instead, every time we observe, there is a new beginning, then the world is creative at the base level."**

What he's saying is that we are creating every moment of our "reality"as we go – with our consciousness – which can be interpreted as our thoughts and ultimately our feelings. Here's a bit more explanation from Goswami;

"Naturally we project that the moon is always there in space-time, even when we are not looking. Quantum physics says no. When we are not looking, the moon's possibility wave spreads, albeit by a minuscule amount. When we look, the wave collapses instantly; thus the wave could not be in space-time...There is no object in space-time without a conscious subject looking at it..."

Don't worry. I'm not going to turn this into a physics treatise. But I want you to realize that the greatest minds of our time, the cutting-edge scientists, are already onto this idea that we have only the foggiest idea of how our "reality" works. Yet they believe that somehow we can change "reality" by interacting with it. I'm not a scientist, but I can tell you from the perspective of a career counselor, that, for whatever reason, these metaphysical principles combined with the practical career exercises in this book (designed to change your way of looking at things) are guaranteed to change your life.

This process of finding your BrilliantWork is really so simple it will make you laugh. As we go through this chapter, I'll guide you to the realization of how fundamentally easy it is to find your joyful work and have a joyful life!

Consider this: **Life is not a smart contest, a beauty contest, or a competency contest. It's an energy contest. The person with the best energy always wins! They get the life they really want.**

Fill 'er up Tip #1: Re-focus Your Thoughts

How do you fill up your energy tank? How do you move from negative energy to positive energy? Here's the first step. It's all in your head...

Your mind is your best friend and your worse enemy. In western culture we believe we ARE our minds. In Eastern traditions such as Buddhism and Hinduism, the mind is called a chattering "monkey" because it flits from thought to thought uncontrollably causing mischief. The practice of meditation is about learning to control those thoughts. To control the passions, one must control the mind, says the Dalai Lama. You may already realize that the first step to any kind of happiness or success is learning to control those thoughts. What's the reason for this?

Because our thoughts control our feelings. And our feelings create our world – going back to our quantum physics theory. We are electro-magnetic beings, vibrating constantly, and those vibrations are creating our "reality."

"The wise man in the storm prays to God not for safety from danger, but for deliverance from fear."

Ralph Waldo Emerson

Now why would Emerson say that? **Because, like it or not, that fear you're feeling in the midst of the storm is pulling the storm into your life…**

In Christianity, prayer is the art of focusing the mind on positive intent, on a productive dialogue with God. This is yet another technique for controlling negative thoughts. In new age spirituality, a lot of attention is given to the power of affirmations.

These affirmations are sentences that voice our belief in a positive outcome. They're intention statements used to focus our wills in a positive direction. Here's one example: *"I will soon find joyful work that I'll love doing, and it will support my family financially."*

In a speech given by His Holiness the Dalai Lama in Washington, D.C. (November 8, 1998) he explained:
"If you let negative emotions and thoughts arise inside you without any sense of restraint, without any mindfulness of their negativity, then in a sense you are giving them free reign. They can then develop to the point where there is simply no way to counter them. However, if you develop mindfulness of their negativity, then when they occur, you will be able to stamp them out as soon as they arise. You will not give them the opportunity or the space to develop into full-blown negative emotional thoughts … "
His Holiness the Dalai Lama

It's the mind's job to caution you against taking risks in your life. The mind is trying to preserve your life – to stop you from doing anything that could threaten your existence. In the past, those warnings of danger involved staying away from predators and not walking off the edge of a cliff.

In modern society, our dangers are much more subtle. The mind is still doing its job very well when it sends you fear thoughts as you consider taking a brave step forward. Your job is to listen to those negative thoughts and carefully turn them around with positive thoughts. Or those negative thoughts will sabotage all your best efforts to have a good life.

Imagine if the only thing stopping you from having the life you want is your negative thinking – not the limited resources or abusive family members or the millions of other excuses you come up with for not having a successful life.

Following along the lines of the Dalai Lama's teachings, I've written a few positive affirmations to help you turn around your negative thoughts and beliefs.

Five daily career affirmations

1. With each breath I take, I choose joy over fear.

2. When I feel fear, I act courageously.

3. I am being guided at this moment to find joyful work that will support me in every aspect of my life.

4. My circumstances no longer affect me; I affect my circumstances.

5. I intend to find joyful work.

Let's take the Dalai Lama's teachings a bit further...

We often spend our time mulling over problems. We focus on what's wrong in our lives constantly – thinking that somehow this will make things better. It's a law of quantum physics that what we focus on gets bigger. Thus, simply by becoming aware of what we're thinking about and switching it to a focus on solutions – we can solve our "impossible" problems.

Today, each time you find yourself thinking about problems, instantly switch your focus to solutions. Get a notebook and on the cover of it write "Solutions." Inside write the three biggest problems facing you right now. Keep this notebook with you all day. When you find yourself thinking about problems, pull it out and jot down at least three possible (even funny) solutions to the problem. This retrains your monkey mind to focus on solutions.

Soon you'll have a notebook full of solutions. As you read through these wonderful, crazy, funny, creative ideas you've written, you'll get a new perspective on your life. This is the beginning of your journey to a more fulfilling life and more prosperous career. Here's an example:

Problem:
I can't find a job that I love.

Solutions:
I intend to research owning a franchise.
I intend to look into going back to school.
I intend to finish the BrilliantWork program and find
my true career.
I will research joining the Peace Corps.

It's just as important to recognize your negative **beliefs** and turn those around immediately. When you constantly think, "Well, it doesn't matter how hard I work, I never get recognition," the universal source feels that low-end vibration belief and provides you abundantly with more of the same negative energy to match what you're sending out. The first step is recognizing your negative beliefs.

The tricky thing about this is that we live in a very negatively-oriented world. If you listen to conversations around you,

or watch the news, you'll notice that most discussions have a negative focus. Things are grim and getting grimmer, according to just about everybody. Anyone with a positive attitude and a focus on solutions stands out like a light bulb in a dark room. When you accept this group-consciousness of negativity (and the beliefs that go along with it such as "there's never enough money; life is very hard; nobody gets a great life unless they're selfish and bad; everyone gets sick") you are accepting a very limited view of life. Thus you will have a very limited life – with little happiness. It's your choice. What you believe is what you get.

The first step is to become an observer of your mind. Whenever you hear a negative belief crossing your mind – instantly turn it around. In your "solutions" notebook, write three of your negative beliefs. Next to them, write positive antidotes.

Negative belief:

1. No matter how hard I work, I never make enough money.
2. The economy is so bad and there aren't any jobs.

Positive Antidote:

1. I intend to work with inspiration from the high-end of my continuum; I'll be recognized and abundance will flow into my life.
2. When I look for a job while using my high-end energy, I'll attract wonderful opportunities into my life.

Just by thinking of something that makes you feel joy or gratitude and makes you vibrate at a higher level, you're aligning yourself with forces that will bring more joy and happiness into your life. This is the power of affirmations. But most importantly, they change your feelings – which changes your world.

Amit Goswami, Ph.D., explains this in the book I mentioned earlier. He contends, and this is very important to understand, that "reality" is not a static, objective state, according to quantum physics. He contends that it is mutable, and in fact, being created by the observer – which is you!

By believing you can find work you love, seeing that work, and even feeling that joyful life before you have it, you are changing this objective "reality" and creating the new reality based on your beliefs, thoughts and feelings.

In this book, you will do many exercises that help you identify your innate talents, passions and dreams. You will get a clear picture of what type of work you would be happy doing. Then you will learn to add your positive energy into the recipe for success.

Here's the secret ingredient that determines your success...Energy!

While doing all the exercises in this book which help you identify what you truly long to do with your career, you must also raise your vibrations (by feeling joy, love, divinity, inspiration, etc.) so that you can attract new opportunities into your life.

Fill 'er up Tip #2: Move Your Energy

Your first question each morning should be:

"Where am I on my energy continuum?"

Kevin's Story

Kevin first came to me as a client looking for career counseling. He was a software engineer at a large corporation and he hated his job. Yet he had three kids to support, and we were in the midst of the bad economy of 2002.

"There just aren't any other jobs out there right now for software engineers," he said miserably during our first session. I took Kevin through the career exercises you'll find in this book. These essential exercises helped him peel back the layers to see what he really longed to do – his BrilliantWork – which was growing orchids, creating a computerized system that perfectly controlled their growing environment, and selling these orchids to retailers and consumers from his website.

Once we uncovered his BrilliantWork, he became more frustrated. "Now I know what I truly long to do, and yet it seems impossible," he said. That's when our real work began. I began guiding Kevin to understand the physics of how he was attracting things into his life. We discussed physics, the laws of attraction, and that we are all electromagnetic beings – attracting things, events and people to us constantly.

I asked him to give me one day as an energy experiment.

I asked him to wake up the next day and before getting out of bed to imagine that two million dollars were dumped into his bank account. I asked him to picture how his life would change. To see the new greenhouse he would build, to see and smell all the awesome orchids growing in it, to imagine his family helping him run the business. I told him to go about the entire day feeling as if he had this wonderful new life. He was to interact with everyone, do every task of the day, as if he now owned and ran a successful orchid business, had more than enough money to have the life he wanted, and was truly joyful.

It was an experiment, I explained, to see what he could attract into his life in one day of shifting his energy as if he already had the life he wanted.

Kevin, who had always been a very passionate person, found it easy to feel the feelings involved in having his dream come true. He began acting and feeling as if he were already filled with joy and already had his new career. By the end of the week, Kevin had been laid off from the job he hated, and had a lucrative job offer to work as a computer consultant for a small company where he was honored and appreciated for his talents. This consulting work gave him the money and time he needed to build his orchid business. Today, Kevin has a new life. He not only transformed his career, but every relationship in his life as well. "Thank you for showing me how to get it," he says. "What you did was sort of like showing me how to turn away from the dark side of the force. I'm thankful everyday."

Throughout this book, I'll give you more specific ways of changing your vibration level by improving your feelings – to improve your life.

Here's another important piece in the puzzle to improving your vibration level and reinventing your life and career...

Fill 'er up Tip #3: Ignore Your Belittler

"No one can make you feel inferior without your consent."

Eleanor Roosevelt

Your mind is your greatest enemy to finding work you'll love. The mind is threatened by change, and it projects fear in the form of: "Who do you think you are? You should just get a job, any job." This is the voice of your belittler, and you must choose to graciously ignore it.

All of us have grown up with someone doubting our abilities. It's a law of human nature that someone in our lives will doubt us. If it wasn't your mother, perhaps it was your father, or another relative. These people tell us that we "screw up" everything we do. They say, "Who do you think you are? Just get a job, any job." This implies that we have no unique talents or gifts, and therefore should fit into any slot we try to slip into.

We have the power and the responsibility to graciously ignore those voices. The beauty of being human is the ability to make choices. Choose not to be belittled! It's not what someone says that matters, it's what we do with that information that determines if it will harm us. If we focus on it, it can ruin us. Then we have given control of our lives over to our belittler (and our negativity). When we choose to ignore the belittler, we are in control of our lives.

Recognize that your soul chose to have this person in your life – for a reason. The negative message this belittler is sending you is a negative belief that you long to eradicate in your life. Only by having it forced upon you, will you find the strength to break your pattern of believing it. This negative person in your life is actually doing an important job helping you improve your life and find your power. Be grateful for them.

I had a client whose mother was her belittler. When this client was laid off from her job at a large corporation (along with 7,000 other people), her mother said, "I'm amazed that with your wonderful education and your high intelligence, you can't figure out how to get along with your bosses."

I took this client through an exercise that she found very helpful. I'd like to share it with you.

Sending Them to Bed Without Any Dinner

1. Relax, get comfortable, turn off any background noise, and take a deep breath.

2. **Imagine one of the proudest moments of your life.** This could be recent or an event from your childhood. It could be graduating from high school, getting good grades, performing in a play, getting a promotion, writing a book, etc.

3. Remember that moment and all the praise you received. During that time, **did anyone in your life say something that deeply hurt your feelings?** If so, I'm sure you remember it. Think of it now and remember who said it to you. Picture that person.

4. Look that person in the eyes and say with love and graciousness, **"You may not speak to me that way again. I'm sending you to bed without any dinner."**

5. Visualize that person slinking off to their bedroom feeling humbled and acting as if they got your message and will never talk to you that way again.

6. When you think of this person from now on, picture them slinking off to bed without any dinner. **They are no longer powerful in your mind.** You are no longer intimidated by them. The words they say no longer have impact on you.

7. Picture that person crying in their room. **Go to them, and love and soothe them.** Hold them in your arms and comfort them. You are now their protector and nurturer, because you realize how they need love to become better, kinder human beings. Feel compassion for them and for their life story.

8. Slowly come out of your visualization. From now on **when you think of that person, you are comforting them, nurturing them, and soothing them.** They are like a child in need of your love. This is the only way you will think of them from now on.

9. Whenever this person says something hurtful to you, think this thought: **I recognize your great need for love, and I offer you love and compassion.** If you are Christian, you will recognize the words Jesus said: "Father forgive them, for they know not what they do."

10. Write down all the thoughts and emotions you experienced during this exercise. Do this visualization for several days until you find yourself thinking of that person in a new way.

11. Whenever you hear a voice in your brain saying something belittling and hurtful to you, respond by saying, **"Oh, that's the voice of _____. Poor thing. S/he just needs some love."**

Write down 2 people in your life who have been your "belittlers."
Do the exercise with each of them in mind.
Write down your responses.

Here are some affirmations for quieting your belittler:

1. Who do I think I am? I'm me and that's good enough.

2. I will just get a job, and it will be a job I love.

3. I do everything in my life to the best of my ability and for the highest good.

4. I am unique, and my unique style guides me to the perfect expression of my soul through my work.

One of the most powerful exercises I do with my clients is taking them through the *Getting Centered Exercise* described below. This could be the most powerful step you take towards finding your joyful work. Please give it a try.

Getting Centered Exercise:

It's essential to our well-being that we learn to quiet the mind and control our thoughts. The most essential part of us – our souls, spirits, inner selves (use whatever term you prefer) is much deeper inside of us than our thoughts. **We are not our thoughts.**

When we need to get clarity, to make major decisions about our lives, we need to access this deeper part of ourselves which is always connected to the divine. The following exercise will help you access that place.

1. All of us have known the experience of feeling grounded, centered and calm. We may have experienced this state during exercise, sport competitions, meditation, prayer or even when being with a loved one. Right now, **sit with your feet flat on the floor** so you can feel your connection to the earth.

2. Sit with your spine straight and **put your hand on your abdomen** with the thumb on your bellybutton and the rest of the hand below your belly button.

3. **Take three deep breaths.** As you inhale, feel this area of your abdomen expand. As you exhale, feel it contract.

4. **This is your center, your place of knowingness.** In western culture we put great emphasis on the chatter that goes on in our minds day after day. In eastern cultures, they call this the Monkey Mind. Meditation teaches us to step back from these thoughts, observe them, and control them.

5. **The center is our place of greatest power.** It is the place we can move from with certainty that we are going in the right direction. For example, when you study martial arts, karate, judo, tai chi, even dance, you learn to move from this place of center. When you are

standing in a room and four opponents attack you from four different corners of the room, if you are in touch with your center, you know exactly which way to turn to face your opponents.

6. When you move from that place of center, **you can't be thrown off balance.** You are poised, balanced, grounded, unshakeable; and you don't care beans what anyone thinks about you.

7. Now, try to **remember a time in your life, when you were very centered**, powerful, grounded, fearless. You knew exactly what to do and when to do it. Picture that time in your memory. What was your breathing like? What did your voice sound like? How did your body feel? Try to remember any cues that might help you regain that state whenever you choose it.

8. For example, when I walk or hike, **my feet feel very heavy**, very connected to the earth. It helps me get into my centered state when I walk or pace and feel my feet heavy against the earth. Find a memory cue in your body that helps you get into your center easily.

9. In that state of calm, spend ten minutes silently repeating one word such as Om or Peace or Jesus. Watch the thoughts that flit across your mind. Gently bring your attention back to the repeated word whenever you notice your mind wandering. After ten minutes, take three deep breaths and stop repeating the word.

10. Now from that place of center, of knowingness, ask yourself the following three questions:

   What is the joyful work that would make me happy and support me in every way?

   What steps do I need to take now to make it happen?

   What can I do to remove the obstacles that are preventing me from doing this work?

11. **As you bring yourself back to waking awareness, write down your responses to the questions above. Spend several minutes writing and reflecting on your experience before getting up and going about your day.**

– What insights have I gained about the nature of my mind?

– What insights have I gained into my "belittler voice"?

– How is my belittler stopping me from finding work I love?

– How can I use the power of my positive energy to overcome this obstacle?

Fill 'er Up Tip #4: Go on a Diet of the Heart

You must go on a diet of the heart in order to succeed at finding the work you'll love. This diet only allows positive emotions – no fear, self-doubt, anger and blame – just joy, courage and determination.

In the award-winning movie, *A Beautiful Mind*, based on the life of mathematician and Nobel Prize Winner, John Nash, someone asks Nash, late in his life, if he's still crazy and still has delusions. He answers: "I still have delusions. I'm still crazy. Sanity is just a diet of the mind. I choose not to indulge certain appetites. I choose which thoughts to follow and which thoughts to ignore."

That inspiring movie illustrates the human struggle that all of us deal with everyday of our lives. We choose sanity over insanity, courage over fear, love over hate, each moment of our lives, with each thought we choose to follow, with each thought we choose to ignore.

When I work with my clients, this is one of the primary principles that governs their success as they search for joyful work.

Here's one example:

Lynne's Story

Lynne sat cross-legged in her chair, arms crossed, staring me down. "I started to pursue this new line of work that we've come up with...But I became paralyzed," she explained to me.

"Every time I tried to pick up the phone to do the networking calls you suggested, a voice inside of me said, 'You're crazy. You fail at everything. You're inept. Don't waste your time on this. Just go get a minimum-wage job. Get security. You'll fail at this new stuff. Who do you think you are anyway?'"

I explained to Lynne that this voice is the voice of her "belittler." It may have come from her parents, or from anyone who has had power in her life. "Your challenge is to hear that voice, make friends with it and say, 'Oh, I knew you'd say that. You always say the same thing. But you know what? I'm going to pursue this new direction anyway. Thank you very much.' And then have a great laugh, go about your business, and do it anyway."

I played the two million dollar game with Lynne and asked her to imagine her life with two million dollars in her bank account.

She sighed a huge sigh of relief and explained in great detail her dream of starting a non-profit organization where she could help single moms get legal and financial support to improve their lives. She pictured herself being like a "nurturing grandmother" to these women in transition – providing them with services and support and receiving joy and gratitude in return. She noticed the huge shift in her energy (from negative to positive) when she imagined having the life she wanted.

Lynne also wrote down word-for-word what I had told her to say to the voice in her head. We discussed how listening to that fear voice inside of her made it stronger, gave it energy, and made it get more powerful. "The more often you ignore it, thank it for the input, and then go about doing your work anyway, the weaker that voice will get. And humor is a great antidote to fear. Whenever you hear that little fear voice, give a great big joyful laugh out loud, and it will begin to go away."

Her homework that week was to get informational and networking interviews lined up with three Social Services employees in order to learn more about changing her career in that direction (and getting away from retail department store jobs).

The next week she showed up for her appointment with a huge smile on her face, and leaned back on the couch looking calm and at ease. "I've done it," she said grinning. "I've got FIVE interviews lined up. The first time that voice really tried to stop me and I just laughed at it. It's so familiar to me. It's like an old friend. So I laughed at it and picked up the phone and made the call anyway. I got the interview! Then I started feeling cocky and wanted to see how many interviews I could line up – more than we expected. It went beautifully. By the time, I made my last call, the little fear voice was barely a whisper and very easy to ignore."

By using her dream of running her own non-profit organization as the fuel that got her joy going each morning, Lynne found a job in Social Services doing intake interviews with clients.

She felt needed, appreciated, and that she was doing something to help the world. It was a huge improvement for her self-esteem.

Meanwhile, she enrolled in an adult college offering evening classes towards getting her Masters in Social Work. As of now, this single mom with three kids is supporting her family by working at a job that has meaning for her, and enjoying her evening classes which are taking her career in a better direction. She has also begun networking with non-profit experts and creating the business plan that will help her start her own non-profit. More doors are opening for her everyday.

How powerful this Diet of the Heart can be...

When I was going through my second major life/career change, I was a single mom with very little money. I had lost 4 high-paying Internet jobs when the Internet fell apart. I couldn't get a job anywhere. I went to see a career counselor and began the search that led me to start my own business. When I started my own business, everyone told me I was crazy to do such a risky venture with a child to support and no savings. Everyone said it would take years to build my business. The only choice I had was to make my business highly successful almost overnight.

After awhile, I began to believe that they were right; that it was indeed impossible. My negative thoughts began to sabotage all of my efforts. Eventually, my bank account was empty and I was in grave debt. Then I went through a major energy transformation which I described in the beginning of this chapter. After my transforming moment, I went on a strict Diet of the Heart. At 2 AM every morning, I would wake up in fear at the thought of losing my home, ruining my daughter's life, etc.

At those moments, I learned to discipline my feelings – I would play the two-million dollar game with myself and see every detail of the life my daughter and I would have when my business was ridiculously financially successful. I would see it and see it until the joy of the images made me giggle.

Then I would watch a favorite comedy on TV and settle down to do some laughing out loud – at 2 AM. Wow! Nothing improves your attitude and emotions more than a great comedy. After laughing for an hour and feeling joy and gratitude for all the gifted comedy actors and film directors in the world, suddenly I'd get new ideas for my business and they would come to me with joy – rather than desperation. And those joyfully inspired ideas always proved to be greatly successful.

On one of those sleepless nights, I sat with a pad of paper and pen in my hand and waited for guidance. Within 10 minutes, all of my Seven

Secret Steps had literally poured onto the pages of my notebook. Those ideas brought countless visitors to my website, numerous clients to my counseling business, and eventually led to my first book. I'll bet this Diet can do amazing things in your life.

Write down your reflections on how the Diet of the Heart can help you:

Here are some questions to answer:

What would my life look and feel like if I had two million dollars in my bank account right now?

What is my real, unspeakable, barely imaginable dream career?

When you see this career in detail, notice that happy feeling in your heart. Hold on to that feeling. That's the secret ingredient to making your dreams come true.

Here are 8 ways to quiet the fear voice in your mind. This is your new diet.

1. **Learn to recognize a fear thought and distinguish it from a healthy thought.** Many people go through life not even understanding the effects their thoughts have. They don't realize that they can control those thoughts and thus control their moods. For example, someone will say, "I'm having a bad day" or "I'm in a bad mood." If you pay attention to your thoughts, step back and observe them, you begin to see that they are mostly fear statements when you're in a "bad mood." When you're having a great day, your thoughts are telling you things will be okay, people love you, etc. The enlightened ones amongst us recognize this process and learn to control their own thoughts thus controlling their destinies. However, the first step is recognition.

2. **When you have fear thoughts**, thank them for inspiring you to overcome something. They're making your personal challenge very clear. Feel gratitude! Then turn them around with positive intention, "I intend to…"

3. Hold the **Ultimate Dream** in your mind. Write it on a piece of paper and tape it to your bathroom mirror. This ultimate goal is: **I will find work that serves the world in a meaningful way, serves my spirit in a joyful way, brings me happiness, and supports me financially.** Now build out that goal in great detail. What house will you live in when you are financially successful from doing work you love? Picture it and feel that giddy joy in your heart from seeing the life you want. USE THAT FEELING as your ally everyday!

4. When your fear thoughts are overwhelming, **drown them out with prayer**, mantra, or a word/phrase that has a positive meaning for you

such as Peace be with me. If you intentionally fill your mind with joyful or positive thoughts, there isn't room for the fear. You can also use a wonderful memory that fills you with peace and happiness. Work with it until you feel your emotions shift to happiness. It's easier than you think. And try some loud, uninhibited rip-roaring laughter. When you get to that point, you've turned the corner and your emotions will begin to bring you what you truly want.

5.   Picture one person in your life (dead or alive) (your child, your father, your guru, etc) whom you love with all your heart. Tell yourself that you're going to do your best to **overcome these frightening obstacles for that person**. Feel the love in your heart for the person. Let it envelop you. Fear cannot exist in your heart simultaneously with love. Choose the love.

6.   Acknowledge that you may not be able to manifest the perfect job tomorrow. But **new doors will open, and new possibilities will reveal themselves to you simply because you are putting out good effort and energy.** These positive results will come to you because you are moving forward courageously and thus attracting them with your higher energy vibrations. New possibilities won't come when you're retreating to old patterns of fear and stagnation. Remember, it's all physics.

7.   Eliminate or greatly **reduce the "high-fat" foods/thoughts from your Diet of the Heart.** For example, avoid movies, TV shows, music, books, or situations that fill you with fear and anxiety. Choose your entertainment for its ability to inspire you and give you courage. My best girlfriend cannot watch a very popular hospital television series because it fills her mind with fear of terrible things happening to her family. Television and movies have enormous impact on our psychic systems. They build images inside of us that may never be

erased. Choose carefully the images you want imprinted on your brain. ALWAYS choose comedies and inspiring movies over fear-based dramas. Avoid news whenever possible.

8. **Design your feel-better plan and write it down.** When the fear hits, say, okay, first I'll think of that wonderful snorkeling trip I took to Mexico and I'll feel the peace of swimming in that warm water. Then I'll see my daughter performing her version of a pop/rock song, and I'll start to giggle and smile. Then I'll picture the new house I'm going to buy for my family with my fabulous new income. Then I'll do 30 minutes of exercise. Then I'll watch a comedy to make myself laugh. Then I'll just start laughing out loud over how simple life really is, in spite of everything. We're just supposed to feel happy...what a great cosmic joke!

Write down your feel-better plan.

Fill 'er Up Tip #5: Use EPR:
Energetic Personal Resuscitation

When I teach my classes and workshops, my students love learning EPR. It's a quick easy technique for switching energy to a higher frequency. These three quick emergency switches for improving your energy are **humor, gratitude and sweetness**.

You can use these energy-saving techniques quickly and effectively in any emergency situation where your energy is at the lower end of your continuum. By switching to any one of these feelings, you'll rise higher on your continuum and thus be better able to respond to the crisis.

Why does this work?

Humor is a very quick way to easily tap into source energy. When we laugh with big, open-hearted, unrestrained laughter, we are recognizing the absurdity of life. We start to see the big picture. We start connecting.

Gratitude is a high-vibration feeling. When you get it pulsing through you, you'll feel opened up and receptive to source energy. Gratitude works especially well to counteract anger. By sending this high-level emotion to someone you have conflict with, the conflict will begin to soften. You will no longer be a victim to this relationship.

Sweetness: When we show our true sweet selves to others, they open up and show us their sweetness. It's like holding a baby. We see the sweetness and go there to join it. If we switch to sweetness in the midst of conflict, we'll see instant positive results and a better resolution. Try it!

Today, try using EPR in a tight situation. If you're waiting in line at the post office and the long wait is driving you crazy, use EPR to improve your energy – which will instantly improve the situation.

In your solutions notebook, write an example of a time when you successfully improved a difficult situation by using EPR. Make a habit of using EPR everyday when you would normally react to a situation with anger, fear, or other forms of negativity.

Exercises for the Mind & Heart

1. When your mind says, "You should just get a job, any job." Your reply is: **I will happily get a job** – the perfect job for me.
    And laugh out loud!

2. When your mind says, "Who do you think you are?" You reply:
    I'm me and that's good enough!

3. Your mind controls how you feel about things, therefore **controlling your mind** breath-by-breath controls how you feel and act. Think of a favorite comedy scene from a movie you love. See it until you start giggling. Giggle until you feel happy. Notice how quickly you improved your vibration level.

4. **Imagine a perfect day** in the life of a perfect career. See it start to finish – even if it seems impossible. Write down exactly what you saw and why you liked it. Now describe it out loud and talk about it until you're smiling and getting the joy feeling inside. Walk around the house talking out loud about this perfect new career you're going to have. Laugh about how ridiculously happy you're going to be doing this work.

5. **Start each morning by sitting for 20 minutes** and repeating a word of your choosing. It could be a Christian word such as Jesus or "peace"or it could be the Hindu word Om. As your mind wanders, gently bring it back to that word – without tension. Be gentle. Watch the thoughts go by. When the mind is quiet, **start pumping in the joy**. See the perfect dream vacation you're going to take your family on. See their faces when you tell them you've bought the tickets. Hold that feeling and build on it.

6. Start each morning **reading from a spiritual book** such as the bible, or the scriptures from your particular spiritual path. Go for that feeling of peaceful contentment. Read until you FEEL that everything will be alright no matter what. Ask for guidance. There is always help available from the other realms. Call in the light. Say God's name in whatever religion you follow.

7. Start each day by **visualizing a perfect day** from beginning to end. Take at least five minutes to see it clearly from what you'll wear to work that day to how easily you'll get your work done, to how well the meeting will go. Imagine friends asking you out for dinner and getting an unexpected check in the mail. Do this until you feel the joy. Carry that feeling with you for the rest of the day.

8. Choose one of the **positive career affirmations** written in this workbook and repeat it throughout the day watching how it improves your feelings...and your vibration level.

ARE YOU GETTING THIS GREAT COSMIC JOKE?

If you want happiness, all you have to do is feel happy...

If you want your dreams to come true, all you have to do is pretend that they already have...

It's so simple, it's funny!

And we don't see it because we're addicted to our struggles – to our limited view of what "reality" is.

Chapter Two

Dream

Your dreams (both waking and sleeping) are your keys to happiness; What do you really want?

"Nothing happens unless first a dream."
Carl Sandburg

Your dreams are essential for identifying your BrilliantWork and attracting it into your life. Here's the joke: We're told from the time we're children to stop dreaming, to get our heads out of the clouds, and to face reality. **Yet dreaming creates reality.** Our dreams make us feel happy, and thus raise our energy levels so that we attract good things into our lives.

This may be a bit confusing, so I'll break it down. When you were growing up you probably had countless dreams of what you wanted to "be" when you grew up. You may have wanted to be a Hollywood film director. However, you obediently listened to your elders who told you that dream was impossible and you should get a realistic career – such as being a software engineer or a lawyer.

Years went by and you stuffed away your film-director dreams – never even mentioned them to anybody again. You dutifully became a software engineer because you believed that our world is ruled by a fixed reality. This fixed reality, you were told, says that hardly anybody ever really gets to live their dreams – especially if they're dreams of great success and financial abundance. Eventually, you became a **miserable** software engineer because being a software engineer didn't utilize your innate talents of creativity or story telling. Because you were miserable you began taking out your unhappiness on your family and friends. Pretty soon, your whole life was going down the tubes – simply because you were unhappy – simply because you didn't follow your dreams.

You go see a career counselor. If it's a good career counselor, the first thing they ask is "What are your dreams? What do you long to do?" Suddenly, for the first time in years, you get in touch with that old Hollywood dream. You dig it up and start talking about it, laughing about it, seeing yourself being a film director, feeling what that career would feel like. You imagine yourself giving directions to Julia Roberts or Al Pacino. See them asking for your advice about a scene. You do this until you are giggling about how much fun this career would be – until you feel the joy you would have in this work.

Immediately, you experience a shift of energy. You feel happy as you imagine your dream. Because you're happy, you begin attracting happier events, opportunities and people into your life. You now function mostly from the high–end of your continuum. You research schools that offer courses in film directing and editing. You check out a book from the library about careers in the film or TV industry. You search the internet. Mostly, you feel the joy of that dream. You allow it to blossom inside of you. One day, you get introduced to a local film-maker who is working on a film that involves your area of expertise. Before you know it, you're interning on a film set and learning the skills you've always wanted to know. Events keep leading to other events, and eventually, you're working in the world of film. Or you attract a job that contains the elements you wanted from film directing – such as being in charge of creating a visually compelling end-product, being the manager of a creative team, and solving problems. Either way, you're much happier in your work and in your life.

Fill 'er Up Tip #6: Dream it BIG to raise your energy!

Because...that high-energy feeling, is your key to attracting what you want as you go about researching careers. That joy will attract the information and the people you need into your life. Use the dream to create the joy. Use the joy to get you vibrating on the level that makes your dreams come true! Remember, without a dream to guide us, our actions and ideas lack inspiration and brilliance.

"Imagination is the true magic carpet."

Norman Vincent Peale

My daughter and I love to go to musicals. One of our favorites is South Pacific. After seeing it recently, we spent days singing this line: "You've got to have a dream, if you don't have a dream, how are you gonna have a dream come true?"

Talking to my daughter reminds me of the power of our dreams. Children have millions of dreams for tomorrow – from the birthday party they want to have, to the costume they'll wear on Halloween, to being a movie star. I encourage my daughter to dream – and to dream big. And I share my dreams with her. Nearly everyday we share our dreams for the future – each encouraging the other to dream bigger.

It's amazing how many people don't allow themselves to dream. Without dreaming of a wonderful career, you won't find one. Once a week, play the $2 million game with yourself. You suddenly have $2 million in your bank account, perfect health, perfect relationships, yet you still have to work. What would you do? What do you really want?

Never face reality!
Face your dreams!
The dreams change your reality!

When my father died, he told me that he regretted not pursuing his dreams. He was a very loving and responsible father who raised four children and provided us with a beautiful home and comfortable lifestyle. We deeply appreciated his sacrifices for us; however we wished he had followed his dreams (such as being a jazz pianist, going on more fishing trips, and owning a beach house). Will your children feel regret for you when you die? Is that what you want for them? Is that the belief system you want to leave to them? "Life is hard and dreams don't come true."

Instead, give them the positive belief that they **can** create a better life, and that dreams do come true. They model their behavior patterns after what you do, not what you say. Everyday you model a belief system about work. Show them that you **can** find your BrilliantWork and have a joyful life. It all starts with dreaming...

By using dreams and visualization, my clients quickly get a "gut" response about whether a new career idea is the right one to pursue. I'm going to teach you that technique in chapter five. It will help you choose which direction to go in.

One of my brightest clients had listed 21 possible careers that she was considering pursuing. Her ideas were endless and seemingly scattered through every major job category from computer programmer to party planner. By having her picture and "feel" a day in the life of each career, she quickly got "no" responses from all except two – which she felt were her Brilliantwork. We created a plan to research both directions, until it was clear which direction was right for this point in her life.

Everyone has the answer to their career search already inside of them – waiting to be heard. Every step you take (such as dreaming and visualizing) to get in touch with that answer will bring you closer to finding your Brilliantwork. Constantly ask yourself, "What do I really want?"

Our sleeping dreams are also powerful tools. When you're going through a life transition, keep a journal next to your bed and write your dreams. When we ask for guidance, our souls send messages to us through our sleeping dreams. After my husband died and I was searching for a new career, I dreamed that a friend handed me a journalism degree and told me to use it. That dream was a turning point in my decision to return to school and study journalism.

At other turning points, I've daydreamed with friends in order to get clarity. I remember staying awake all night with a girlfriend, staring up at the star-filled sky and sharing dreams. We asked thoughtful questions about what we wanted our futures to look like. We entertained each other with elaborate descriptions of homes we wanted to live in, men we wanted to love, success we wanted in our careers, and places we would travel to. We laughed until our stomachs hurt – because our dreams were so outrageous.

The next day, I had more clarity than I'd had in months. Finally, I was able to make powerful decisions to move forward. Dream a little dream everyday. This will help you find your way. As *Muhammad Ali* said,

"The man who has no imagination has no wings."

Encourage your children to dream and imagine. It's therapeutic, it stimulates their creative thinking, and it teaches them to use their imaginations to solve problems. When they're older, their dreams will help them make life transitions. They'll be able to imagine new possibilities and make them happen.

To Dream the Possible Dream

1. For one entire day, take five minutes every hour to dream of a perfect vacation. See where it would be, what you would do, and who you would be with.

2. Write down a recent dream you had while sleeping.

3. What do you think that dream is telling you?

4. Write down a daydream that you remember having when you were younger. (Maybe it was for a beach house or a trip to Europe).

5. Stay up all night sharing dreams for the future with a friend. Dream it big!

My dreams help me understand:

Careers I Keep Considering...

On the list below, **write 10 careers that you've often thought about doing.** They can be silly or serious. The important thing is that you've often thought of them.

After you've made this list, it's essential to do the **Day In The Life** visualization (in Chapter 5) for each career on this list. When you get a "no" response in your body, eliminate that career from this list. When you get a "yes" from your body, pursue that career idea further by taking 3 steps in that direction. The important question is: **"Do I feel happy and excited when I imagine myself doing this work everyday?"**

1.

2.

3.

4.

5.

6.

7.

8.

9.

10.

"Make us happy and you make us good."

Robert Browning

David's Story

David had been a successful computer salesman for 10 years, and he had a comfortable life with his wife and two kids ages 8 and 11. However, things were beginning to fall apart. The job he had loved for many years was now filling him with discontent and anger. Changes in the company he worked for and in the management team he answered to left him feeling out of sync with his work, and unappreciated. He was working exceptionally long hours, his marriage was unraveling, and his kids were "acting out" in negative ways.

I'm just not there for my kids the way I want to be, he explained. "I used to be a fun guy," he said to his wife one day in the car. "Yes, you **used** to be," she replied.

David knew he was in trouble and was alienating his family with his unhappiness. "I've always been the middle man at my company, and that was okay for me. Now it's not. I know I'm miserable, but I have no idea how to make a change," he told me after finding my Brilliantwork website on the Internet. He didn't want to make any changes that would upset his wife and children who had "great lives." I explained that his deep unhappiness was going to hurt his family. He tearfully acknowledged that it was already beginning to happen.

We discussed how his behavior was modeling important work values to his children. "They see me upset when I come home from work, and when I talk to my boss on the phone," he said. David didn't want to give his children the impression that work was something you did only to pay the bills, and not for any deeper meaning or purpose.

Together we went through the process of evaluating his values, talents and needs. **I continually asked him "What do you really want?" We created a "raise your energy plan" that included dreaming, visualizing, daily exercise, and lots of laughter.** For the first time in years, he began to feel joy, and that immediately improved his relationship with his family.

He voiced his long silent dream of being a teacher. However, teaching would not support his family financially in the way he wanted to support them. David had excellent communication and people skills and wanted to do work that focused on those talents.

Eventually he gave birth to a plan for a change in career direction which involved becoming a Human Resource specialist. He attended some certification courses and seminars while still employed at his current business. When a Human Resource Director job opened up nearby, he applied (using the secret ingredient – energy) and he got the job. It involved a salary cut, which he discussed with his family. They all agreed that they wanted a "happy dad" again and were willing to cut expenses.

Now, David spends his days communicating with, listening to, and educating employees. He comes home feeling refreshed and happy to spend time with his family. He works fewer hours and is overall much more satisfied with his life. His family is supporting him completely in this endeavor. "My marriage is better, happier, than it's been for years. And I'm spending much more time with my kids and loving it," he reports.

Because of his increased happiness, he is now attracting great things into his life – which at last report included a significant raise and promotion.

David's story illustrates an essential point: We owe it to our loved ones to find happiness and meaning in our life. They reap the benefits of our happiness, and they pay the price for our misery. If we're spending 85% of our waking hours at a job, we need to feel nurtured and energized by our work, or we come home empty with nothing to give our loved ones.

Finding the right work is not just about you. It's about how you treat those around you. Finding joy in your life is also not just about you...it's about how you're affecting the people who love you.

As you ponder whether it's time for a career change, do an honest assessment of your life. Ask your loved ones how you're doing. Ask them if you seem happy most of the time or not. You can use these five questions below to get a reality check. (Only ask people who are lovingly honest with you and don't have an agenda of wanting to hurt you).

Ask Your Loved Ones for Insight

It's very helpful to ask these questions to three different loved ones so that you get a true sense of perspective:

1. Is my happiness important to you? Why or why not?

2. When I'm unhappy how do I act, and how do I treat you?

3. How do I treat you when I'm truly happy?

4. Do you think of me **right now** as a happy person?

5. **When** do you remember me being most happy?
   Can you describe that time in detail?

6. If you could give me one **gift of insight** about my career, what would you say?

Write their answers to these questions in this BrilliantWork workbook and re-read it whenever you feel afraid of improving your career. It will help you realize that your happiness directly affects your loved ones.

Ten Ways to Get Happy

1. If you hate your job, imagine you already have a career you love. Imagine it until you feel your energy get higher on your continuum.

2. If you've been laid off, use the time to rethink your career direction rather than just rushing down the same path you've been pursuing. Find the joy again!

3. Take a spiritual weekend retreat. Prayer and meditation raise our energy levels and connect us to our divinity and inspiration.

4. Write down three activities/people/movies that make you laugh, and spend time with them.

5. Surround yourself with happy, nurturing people and stay away from negative, angry friends and family.

6. Volunteer for a positive-focused organization where you can make a difference in one person's life.

7. Get exercise every day for 30 minutes. Walk, hike, run, swim, dance, do yoga...

8. Eat foods that energize. (Fresh vegetables, protein, and unprocessed foods)

9. Start each day with a prayer or peaceful meditation.

10. Do something wonderful that you're terrified of doing.

Am I truly happy right now?

What do I really want?

How am I affecting my loved ones?

What do I intend to do about it?

OPEN YOUR MIND

Pretend that two million dollars have been dumped
into your bank account.
Picture what your life would be like with that money.
Take a deep breath and feel the freedom of your new life.
See the details of the vacation you would take,
and the joyful work you would do
(after you got bored from vacationing).
Spend a day feeling and acting as if this is already your reality.

Fill 'er Up Tip #7: Find out what you really want
by playing your life backwards...
from end to beginning.

At the end of your life, when you reflect on what really mattered, the people you loved will matter most. Whether or not your work contributed something good to the world will matter second.

"Success has nothing to do with what you gain in life or accomplish for yourself...It's what you do for others." Danny Thomas

My saddest memory is of helping my husband, Paul, reflect on his life as he faced death at the age of 35. This was followed by a similar process with my best childhood girlfriend, Crissie, when she died from leukemia two years later – at the age of 32.

Paul and Crissie were very much alike. They were exceptionally bright, gifted, and talented, and neither of them had found their BrilliantWork. Crissie had become a professional student and was getting a Ph.D. in biology. When she died, besides remembering those she loved dearly, she felt she had failed to find her Brilliantwork; and this caused her great pain.

Paul went through the same thing. He had a Masters Degree in Divinity, had been a taxicab driver, mountaineering instructor, and owner of a T-shirt printing business. He didn't feel that he had ever found his Brilliantwork. I spent hours helping Paul process his dreams and ideas for a new career, but he was never able to manifest them. Crissie went through the same painful process.

When they died, I felt driven to launch myself passionately into meaningful work – which was, at the time, being an editor in the natural health arena. I did it with such passion that I became very successful at it.

I thank Paul and Crissie for the wisdom they gave me. I feel them at my side now. They both understood the value of joyful work. They suffered the pain of not having found it. They shared that pain with me in an honest, heartfelt way that spurred my personal growth.

"Why stay we on the earth except to grow?"
Robert Browning

Much of my passion for helping people find their true work clearly comes from my experiences with Paul and Crissie. Isn't it better for us to search now to find our way, rather than reflect back at the end of our life with regrets?

Make an entry in your "solutions notebook" called **Life Stories of Those I Admire**. Write about the three people in your life who have inspired you most, and how they lived their lives. Compare yourself to them.

3 People I admire and what I most admire about them

1.

2.

3.

10 Questions to ask before you get to the Pearly Gates:

1. What am I most ashamed of?

2. How can I change that right now?

3. What am I most proud of?

4. How can I do something that wonderful again?

5. How will my friends speak of me when I'm gone?

6. How can I improve that right now?

7. What has been the mission of my life?

8. What parts of it have I done well?

9. What have I offered to the world through my work?

10. How can I do better – starting today?

The Old Obit Revisited

1. Write an obituary for yourself as if you died 20 years or more from today. Write it as if the final 20 years of your life were the most productive and successful.

2. Ask a loved one or true friend to write an obit as if you died today. Read it as an honest appraisal of how you've done so far.

3. Write an imaginary obit for yourself as if you've lived a charmed life and had a dream career for your entire life. What can you learn from reading it?

It's enlightening to spend a little time imagining that you're at the end of your life and reflecting back on your accomplishments. What regrets would you have? Would you be proud of the moments when you were courageous about making changes in your life and lived from the high-end of your continuum? Would you be disappointed if you spent your life working at jobs you disliked and being unhappy? These questions get at our core values. They help us see what we really want.

Write your thoughts about what you're proudest of in your life.

Write three dreams you WILL manifest before you die.

Chapter Three

SEARCH

**Find your values, passions, and talents –
Discover what your gifts are.**

Here's another metaphysical joke for you: You're searching for work that will feel joyful and bring you financial abundance. You're trying to be "realistic" as you research careers and evaluate your skills. You're working hard at finding the right answer. Yet it's much easier than you think...**The answer is only a daydream away.**

The only question worth asking is: **"What do I really long to do?"**

Since we aren't in the habit of allowing ourselves to dream, many of us don't know what we really want. It takes awhile to peel back the layers of what we **should** do – before we can see what we long to do.

In this chapter, I'll take you through a process that ALWAYS works. These exercises are designed to peel back those layers for you. At the end of this chapter, you'll have identified what career you really want and created a plan for attracting it into your life.

Most of you have already taken assessment tests such as the Meyers Briggs and other popular standardized evaluations. Nearly all of my clients come to me armed with results from these tests. Yet these results have not gotten them where they want to go. They're still searching for what they long to do. This chapter contains many unique questions and processes that clearly reveal what your soul is longing to do in this world.

Your Natural Talents

Talents are different from learned skills. You may have learned to run computer software, cook in a restaurant, or do bookkeeping. However, those are skills that you've learned in order to survive, to be employable. Your talents are deeper than that. Talents are the unique, natural gifts that flow easily and gracefully through you. They're your gift to the world.

"I'd rather be a failure at something I enjoy than a success at something I hate."

George Burns

Your work must be a good fit for you and use the innate talents and abilities that come easily to you. Your BrilliantWork feels graceful and is not a constant struggle.

John's Story

John was a 42-year-old insurance salesman who dreaded making cold calls. He enjoyed the part of his job that allowed him to interact with people one-on-one and help them pick out the right insurance plan. However, his job required making cold calls and searching constantly for new customers.

He had grown to dislike this part of his job so intensely that he simply stopped doing it. Without bringing in new customers, his managers were extremely unhappy with his performance, his sales numbers dropped dramatically and he was desperate to find another job. When he called me, he felt trapped in his job, miserable, yet needing a good income to support his family. We spent weeks speaking briefly on the phone and by email as he struggled to decide whether or not to make an appointment for career counseling.

"I just need to get over this, keep my job, and support my family," he would say. Finally, with a performance review on the near horizon, and a terrible fear that he would be fired, he came to see me. He filled out some of my homework assignments which revealed his values, talents, needs and work intentions (included in this chapter). And we began the process that would lead him to his joyful work – work that came naturally and easily to him and was not a day-to-day struggle.

Clearly, John was an introvert doing an extravert's job. That much was painfully clear even to him. When I asked about his "dream" career, he quickly said he had always wanted to be a chiropractor. He wanted to help people improve their health, and he enjoyed working with his hands. He had long envisioned himself running a small chiropractor's office. First he would have to go to school to become a chiropractor.

However, John had a family to support. We decided to identify a job or career path that would be more suited for him now, while he began the process of researching chiropractic schools and the time and money it would take to get that degree.

The more we worked together on his dreams and did visualizations of a day in the life of different careers, the more it became apparent that he would enjoy some type of customer service position where he answered questions, informed and educated consumers, solved problems for them, and yet wasn't selling them something. He was still very interested in working in the health field.

He came up with three jobs to pursue: being a wellness coordinator/Healthcare Counselor at a local hospital was his first choice. Together we arranged his resume to reflect his skills helping and educating people, and solving problems.

The most important work we did was helping him understand how the energy he put out into the world was affecting everything that happened to him. He created a daily plan for

getting his energy to the high-end of his continuum. This included exercise, prayer, laughter and dreaming of the future he wanted. He also learned to use EPR in any difficult situation at home or at work. This plan really worked for him, and soon his energy was at the high-end nearly every day.

Using this newly found energy awareness, he arranged informational interviews at local hospitals to research his new career direction. Each person he met was very impressed by him. "It wasn't my resume they were impressed with. It was me – my energy," commented John. His positive energy attracted great interest at each hospital he visited. Within three months, John had a new job as a Healthcare Counselor & Patient Educator at a local hospital. He was making a salary comparable to the one he made as an insurance salesman.

He spent his days educating patients who needed help transitioning from the hospital to home with a newly diagnosed health condition. He felt that his work was in harmony with his needs and values; he was no longer selling anything. He thrived in his new profession. Since he had made a shift to greater happiness, he began attracting great new things into his life also – including a scholarship and a new job at the chiropractic school he wanted to attend.

His transition from desperation to joy was greatly appreciated by his family, as well as by John. This is just another example that your work should be graceful and not a day-to-day struggle.

"Nature arms each man with some faculty which enables him to do easily some feat impossible to any other." Ralph Waldo Emerson

What is graceful work? In Christianity, to be in a "state of grace" means to be lit with the love of Jesus Christ. In Buddhism and Hinduism it is defined as being in harmony with the natural forces and flows of nature – to be in harmony with the life force, the God force.

Career counselors use the term "graceful" to mean being in harmony with your innate genetic nature so that the skills and tasks required by your job are innate skills and talents that you were born with. I take it a step further. To me, your graceful work is not only fun and easy, it brings your soul's gifts to this world.

When we're in this state of grace, our work, our day-to-day tasks flow from us harmoniously and creatively. This is a very different feeling from using skills that we're good at because we've developed them over the years through great work and effort.

Here's an example from my life: As a journalist, I became a fast typist, an efficient user of word processing software, and a competent copy editor. However, my initial drive was to put words together to inform, educate and inspire. Many years of being a journalist led to competency in editing, word processing, etc. These were not my natural talents. They had come with much work and effort. I was offered numerous jobs to edit other people's books and content because of my acquired skill background.

Whenever I accepted those jobs, they were tortuously tedious and exhausting to do day-after-day. At the end of a day of editing other people's copy, I would be depressed, angry, exhausted, and feeling physically ill (headaches and neck aches were too common). I call this drudgery work – rather than inspired work.

I realized that I had become a writer to educate and inspire and now needed to found another outlet for those needs, which I eventually did as a career counselor. Then I found myself writing again, but writing in order to educate and inspire. I had come full circle using the innate talents and skills that I loved.

"To be what we are, and to become what we are capable of becoming, is the only end of life."

Robert Louis Stevenson

Consider these two scenarios: You've become very good at writing computer code after years of training and work experience. However, spending all day in front of a computer doing only that leaves you bored, exhausted and depressed. You keep doing it for 20 years because it makes a living for you and you're "good at it." Every night for 20 years, you come home grumpy, depressed and exhausted. You suffer, and your family suffers.

Scenario number two: You begin to dream. You identify that the reason you went into writing computer code was because you enjoyed the challenge of creative problem solving that it offered. However, sitting in front of a computer all day eventually did not feel creative or challenging. **You finally allow yourself to give voice to your true dream: to be an FBI agent.**

Now we come to my client's story.

Steve's Story

Steve was the world's unhappiest software engineer. He came to me in search of a new career direction. I kept asking him about his dreams, and he kept denying he had any. Finally, in a very timid voice he said, "I've always dreamed of being an FBI agent."

"Yes, let's talk about THAT," I said eagerly.

And we did.

We spent a lot of time building the dream of what his life would be like as an FBI agent. He could feel excitement in his body as he imagined being on the move, solving problems, feeling adventurous. He began to shift his energy to feel the joy and happiness of already having that career. He even took a small vacation from his job in order to "get happy."

66

When he returned from his vacation, he began the long process of applying to be accepted into the FBI training academy. EVERYONE and every book about that career warned him that it was nearly impossible to get accepted into the academy – especially if he was over 30 – and he was.

So he kept going back to his dream, to his vision, to his happiness. Before every letter, before filling out every form, before every phone call, he shifted to believing he already had the job. We spent hours talking about his energy continuum and how his negative thoughts and beliefs could sabotage his great efforts to become an FBI agent. Did he really want to achieve this "impossible" dream or not? Was he willing to retrain his mind to focus on positive solutions instead of negative, worse-case scenarios? His answer was "Yes!" He became skilled at recognizing his negative energy – mid-thought – and turning it around. He constantly focused on his dreams for the future.

He got accepted into the Academy. Today he's very happy doing his Brilliantwork in the world. His life has improved in numerous ways – including attracting a wonderful new love. He believes that his positive energy was responsible for making his dreams come true.

Which way would you rather spend 85% of your day? Doing a task that bores and depresses you because you're good at it and it makes a living? Or would you prefer using your natural skills and talents in a way that excites and challenges you and also makes a living? It's up to you and your beliefs about what you deserve and what is possible.

"What's important is finding out what works for you."
Henry Moore

Fill 'er Up Tip #8: Identify your Natural Talents
5 Ways to Find Your Talents

1. In this BrilliantWork workbook, **make a list of all the skills or talents** that come naturally to you and which you love doing. For example, if you love talking to people in social situations write that down. That's a natural talent of yours. If you love doing crossword puzzles to solve challenging word problems, write that down. It's a natural talent. Don't list the skills you've acquired over the years through job training or job experience.

2. Make a list of the natural talents that you **recognized in yourself as a child.** Did you love writing in high school? Did you win school competitions for your science projects? All of those things that came innately to us as children offer clues to finding our graceful BrilliantWork. Write them down.

3. **Remember a time when you were very happy accomplishing something.** For example, you might have created a wonderfully successful wedding shower for your sister and everyone raved about your creative ideas, themes, decorations and foods. It was easy for you to do, you felt inspired and happy doing it. Write about that experience. Break it down into the skills that you used. List them. These will be your innate talents. Whenever you consider a job or career, evaluate it by comparing the skills that will be required to the ones that come easily to you such as those you've listed here.

4. This exercise is called **"I love waking up in the morning to..."** Finish the sentence with all the activities that you love doing. For example, I love waking up in the morning to spend the day hiking in the mountains, to go see a play, or take my child to the museum.

When you've completed your list, go through each one and **write the things about that activity that you love.** For example, when I spend the day hiking in the mountains I enjoy being outdoors, getting exercise, feeling inspired by the beauty of nature, reflecting on my life in the solitude, etc. After you have broken each activity down, look for themes running through all the activities you love. Write a couple of paragraphs reflecting on how these themes run through your life and how you might incorporate them into a career you would love.

5. Here's a visualization exercise to do that will help you identify your innate talents. **Picture yourself spending the day** doing a task such as making sales calls, writing computer code, working in a retail store, etc. As you see yourself doing that task, notice if there's tension in your body or if you're relaxed. How do you feel at the end of that day? Depleted? Exhausted? Renewed? Happy? Inspired? Write down your discoveries.

My top three innate talents that I love doing are:

1.

2.

3.

Ten Ways to find Graceful Work

1. **Dream**...imagine what you've always dreamed of doing but may not have given yourself permission to even talk about.

2. Talk about it to a career **coach or true friend** (not a family member who is invested in your personal drama and can't be objective).

3. Identify **five things you love about that dream career.** For example, if you want to be a Hollywood director, what five things would you love about doing that? Write them down.

4. **Picture yourself doing this ideal work** all day. Check in with your body to see if you feel tension anywhere or if you feel relaxed and inspired. If it makes you feel happy, hold on to that vision and that feeling. Spend five minutes each morning "practicing" this vision.

5. Write down **five steps** you can take to begin heading in that direction. For example: Call someone who is currently doing that work and ask how they got started, how they like it, what advice they have for you. Do these five steps in two weeks. No excuses.

6. Imagine yourself at the end of your life, talking about what you regretted? **Would you have regretted** not pursuing this work?

7. Imagine a pretend social situation where you introduce yourself to a group of people as this new movie director? Business entrepreneur? See yourself **interacting with people with this new title.** How does it feel? Would you love to describe yourself that way?

8. When you see yourself **being "graceful,"** how do you look? How do you talk? How do you work? Write down all the images and ideas that come to you around the idea of being graceful.

9. When you think of your most **"ungraceful moments,"** what comes to mind for you? What have been your most ungraceful moments at work and why? Write them down. How and why can your new line of work help you steer clear of those ungraceful moments?

10. All of us have **"impossible dreams"** that we don't even say out loud. Write your impossible dream...and then say it loudly: "I intend to be a professional, successful film actress!" (Never mind that I'm 51)... and say it with great passion until you can giggle and enjoy saying it and picturing it.

   Write your thoughts about the nature of "graceful work" and how that applies to any career you're considering now or to any job you've had in the past:

   Is my current job graceful?

   Does it utilize my natural abilities or only my learned skills?

Your Story

"Do not wish to be anything but what you are."

Saint Francis de Sales

You are unique; the life you've lived up until this moment is not a haphazard string of events, but rather a series of stepping stones bringing your soul to this place, to this moment, to do this work for the world.

The most enlightening aspect of being a career counselor is the gift of hearing my clients' life stories. Again and again, I'm amazed at how unique we all are, how our lives have molded and shaped us, and how different our stories are.

Every event that happens to you, happens for a purpose. Consider the possibility that you chose to have each experience you've had – good or bad – to bring you to this moment. And this moment is exactly where you should be to do your unique work in the world.

One job does not fit everybody. Some people are born computer programmers and others are born teachers. Our work will change forms during our lifetimes. However, our basic natures and talents make us better suited for some jobs than for others.

One of my clients told me with great passion how much he loved making sales. He looked at each sale is a great adventure, an opportunity to serve someone by finding out what they needed and providing it for them.

My next client told me that his sales job was "killing" him, because he was so introverted that he felt he was forcing himself on people in an obnoxious way. He longed for a job where he could work quietly on a computer all day long without many interactions with people. He felt it would be rewarding to write computer code. Today, he writes software and loves doing it.

What is your life story? How have the events of your life brought you to this moment? How have they shaped you? And, how is your fear of failure stopping you from moving forward?

Is Fear of Failure Stopping You?

Each of us defines failure in a very different way. Some of us think that aiming really high and not getting completely where we want to go is a complete failure. Others believe that not trying something at all is the same as failing at it.

"Success is going from failure to failure without loss of enthusiasm."

Sir Winston Churchill

Write down your beliefs about failure. Write down your memories of a big failure in your life. Share this with your friend. Reflect on the role "failure" plays in your life. Ironically, the most successful people in life are often those who have failed most often. How can that be? It's because they're not afraid to try new things, and they're not paralyzed by fear of failure.

By the way, fear of failure is simply FEAR. And fear is at the low-end of your energy continuum. It's your negativity. Whenever you operate from fear of failure, things don't turn out well. You actually attract negativity into your life with your fear.

How did you learn to be afraid of failure? It probably began when you were very young. Your father might have failed at a business venture and that became a family lesson in failure that you've internalized. It may now be crippling you in your career search. You can choose to break that pattern. But first you have to understand the pattern.

By recognizing your fear of failure, you can begin to change it. Put some humor into it. Say to yourself, "Boy, I'm a huge failure at

_____." And then laugh a deep belly laugh. Eventually say that sentence out loud to a friend and laugh with them over it. Take the fear out of failure. It will empower you to greater success.

"To thine own self be true."

Shakespeare – Hamlet

Who amongst us doesn't feel as if we've made countless failures in our life? The most fascinating, brilliant, successful people I know have failed most often, most visibly, and most dramatically. Failures serve a wonderful purpose: They get our attention. They wake us up. It's as if our soul is trying to give us a message and can only get our attention through failure. Once we've survived failure, we get the courage to try something new – go in a new direction. When we've survived failure, we find our courage.

If you've experienced failure, consider yourself blessed. My most challenging clients are the ones who have never experienced a career failure such as losing a job, hating a job, or failing at a business venture. They've missed the tremendous wisdom and new direction we gain when things don't go as we had hoped. These disappointments force us to reevaluate our lives. This process of reevaluation is very healthy and leads to bigger and better things. Without it, we become stagnant.

Telling Your Life Story

It's very powerful to do the following exercise with a friend. Each of you writes the answers to these questions and shares them with each other. You'll be struck by the wonderful differences which illuminate your uniqueness.

1. When I grew up, what kinds of activities were valued in my home? Sports? Or books?

2. When I excelled at _____, I received great praise from my parents.

3. Using only one sheet of paper, write your life story (briefly) emphasizing your "accomplishments" and your "failures." Share this with your partner.

4. When I was growing up, I imagined that if I became a _____, I would have a successful, happy life.

5. My greatest fear while growing up was:

6. My greatest dream while growing up was:

7. My greatest success has been:

8. My greatest failure has been:

9. From reading the life story that I wrote and sharing it with a friend, I can see that these things makes me unique:

This is how my fear of failure affects me:

This is how I will change it for the better:

Make Failure Your New Best Friend

1. Take up a new sport you've never tried before, and laugh every time you do it wrong or have trouble learning it.

2. Take a dance class (if you're not a dancer) such as Ballroom dancing. Laugh every time you make a fool of your self.

3. Write five things you're really, really bad at. Share this list with a friend. Choose one of those things to do with your friend – such as cooking, sharing deepest emotions, etc.

4. Embrace something you've been afraid of. Use it as a teacher in your life. Learn from it and laugh about it. Don't allow yourself to feel "like a failure" because of it.

5. Promise yourself that at least once a month you'll do something you're very bad at and very uncomfortble doing. Once it becomes comfortable and you get good at it, choose something else to do. Use humor to help you through the experience.

Is Fear of Success Stopping You?

Okay, maybe you're aware of how your fear of failure is stopping you. Consider that you may have a fear of success that sabotages you even more. Have you ever thought: "Who do I think I am to want great success and abundant money?" Do you believe that few people ever get true success or happiness – and you're not worthy of being one of them? Have you ever succeeded at something big and then questioned if you were worthy of that achievement?

Our biggest fear is usually the fear of how powerful and magnificent we really are. It's terrifying to believe in our greatness. It goes against every message we've been taught our whole lives. If we follow the belief system we've been raised with – humans are limited beings with limited capacity for happiness – we settle for a "normal" life and limited amounts of EVERYTHING.

Imagine if we truly recognized that we are pieces of divinity with unlimited potential for creation, inspiration, divinity and happiness? Our world would be completely different from the world we live in today. Dare yourself to break out of the low-social-consciousness that governs most of our lives. If you don't believe it – you can't have it. Just say YES!

Write your negative beliefs about what you deserve and what it's okay to have:

1. Only selfish, superficial people make lots of money and have easy lives.

2.

3.

Now write the positive affirmation to reverse that belief:

1. I intend to do my BrilliantWork with such passion that I will attract great wealth and ease into my life and use my wealth to help others.

2.

3.

Fill 'Er Up Tip #9: Find Your Passion:
This is your high-octane fuel.

"It is only with the heart that one can see rightly; what is essential is invisible to the eye."

Antoine De Saint–Exupery

The Little Prince

Close your eyes, take a deep breath, and think of the person you love most in the world. How do you feel when you think of that person? Inspired? Full of joy and contentment? This is the power of love. (You can feel it in your "gut.") This feeling is a key to finding your joyful work.

Remember, it's all physics. We are electromagnetic beings constantly vibrating and attracting things that vibrate at the same frequency. Like attracts like. It's a law of physics.

Your feelings determine how fast you vibrate; and joy and passion are the high-octane burners. Feeling those emotions will send out a vibration so strong and pure it will create a vortex of matching energy that will bring more of the good stuff back into your life.

Therefore, finding your BrilliantWork requires you to first get in touch with your passions, and FEEL them. Those high-energy passions will bring you your joyful work.

So let's get busy finding those passionate feelings. Of course, your first passions will be your loved ones. What other passions do you have? If you could write a book about any subject in the world, what book would you love to write? Name the book. Give it a title and a focus. This tells you where your passions are.

It is a burning of the heart I want
It is this burning I want more
        than anything
It is this burning in the core of the heart
That calls God secretly in the night.

Rumi

As *Henry David Thoreau* wrote:

"Only he is successful in his business who makes that pursuit which affords him the highest pleasure sustain him."

How often have you heard someone say they're searching for their soul mate, so they can find true love and happiness? We should search just as passionately for our true work as we search for our true love. It works the same way. When you act and feel as if you already have what you want (whether it's true love or your BrilliantWork), you will attract it.

One client who found his Brilliantwork explained it this way, "When I wake up in the morning, I can't wait to get to work. It's like the feeling I have when I'm about to spend a romantic weekend with my wife."

"In our life there is a single color, as on an artist's palette, which provides the meaning of life and art. It is the color of love."

Marc Chagall

One client told me that during fast-paced business meetings, sitting at a table with bright and witty co-workers, she felt more alive than at any other time in her life. If you feel this way at work, it means you're in your Brilliantwork. In Oprah Winfrey's biography, she describes her first day of hosting a live television talk show. Instead of feeling afraid, she felt fully alive as if she had finally "come home." Your passions and high-end energy will bring you "home" to your true work and your true life.

The Black Cloud

Lose yourself,
Lose yourself in this love.
When you lose yourself in this love,
You will find everything.

Lose yourself,
Lose yourself.
Escape from the black cloud
That surrounds you.
Then you will see your own light
As radiant as the full moon.

Rumi

"Work and play are words used to describe the same thing under differing conditions."

Mark Twain

Very often I hear these words from clients: "This Monday morning I could hardly get myself to go to work. I knew it was time to make a change." Most of us realize that we shouldn't hate going to work, or that if we do feel that way, we need to change.

However, some people believe that work is something you must do for a living, that it's always a miserable experience, and that we should expect nothing more from it. They live their entire lives hating their jobs, and letting that unhappiness interfere with their relationships. If this is your negative belief about work, you will only attract miserable jobs, and your misery will damage your family life. You get what you believe is possible – nothing more, nothing less. What do you believe is possible for you?

If you're reading this book, it means you already want more than unhappiness for yourself and your loved ones. You may also know that the most successful and wealthy amongst us are the ones who find something they love doing and pursue it passionately. Your work is to recognize your negative thoughts and turn them around with positive affirmations. The moment you recognize negativity, say: "I will find work I love, and I'll feel passionately happy about it, and it will improve the quality of my entire life."

"Success follows doing what you want to do. There is no other way to be successful."

Malcolm Forbes

Fill 'Er Up Tip # 10 : Remember favorite jobs from your past and marinate in the happy memories. Identify the key elements of those jobs and use that information to create your new career.

Try to remember a time in your life when your job was fun and it felt like you were "playing" when you went to work. That may have been your experience in college or during your early 20s – before you got serious about careers. Did you dread going to those jobs? No. You had fun at work.

Think about those previous "fun" jobs. What did you love about them? Make a list of the qualities you loved such as a flexible schedule or sense of teamwork. Use this list as a guide to finding work you love. Here's an example:

A friend of mine had once been an Outward Bound Survival instructor in his 20s. He loved being outdoors and leading groups through the mountains. When he got married and had children, he settled down to a corporate career in order to support his family. As an engineer, he made good money and his family had a nice lifestyle.

When he hit his mid-life crisis, he realized that he hated his job, dreaded going to work, was bored to death, and was taking it out on his family. By doing some creative thinking, he launched a business with a partner that has made him successful and happy. His new company provides corporate leadership training and workshops similar to what he did years ago as an Outward Bound instructor. He takes these groups on outdoor challenge trips – blending his experience as a corporate engineer with his love of adventure, nature, change and travel.

"To love what you do and feel that it matters – how could anything be more fun?"

Katherine Graham

My most successful clients are the ones who are able to clearly state their passions. They are deeply in touch with their spirits and their hearts. Years of ignoring your passions and your feelings can inhibit your ability to hear the truth inside of you. The choices we make in our lives build on themselves. One fearful choice leads to another. Today you can make a courageous choice. You can choose to look at yourself honestly and ask, "What do I really long to do? What do I really want my life to look like?"

Play the two million dollar game...see what dreams surface when you take away the bills and financial stress. If any career were possible and achievable, what would you do for a living? Imagine it, see it, until it burns in your heart. That burning is your fuel for creating a better life.

The exercise below can help you feel your passions. This is especially helpful if you are very cerebral and have been accused of not having a generous heart.

Getting in Touch With Your Passion

1.   Close your eyes, get comfortable, take a deep breath. Sit still and quiet for several minutes.

2.   Imagine a ray of brilliant yellow light emanating from the area around the center of your chest. Picture it as flaming sunlight pouring out of your chest and shining brightly on everything around you.

3.   Hold your hands out, palms facing upwards, in front of your chest. Feel the warmth of that light on your hands.

4.   Imagine that light spreading out to reach all of your house, your family, your street, and your neighbors. See them basking in it. See them feeling loved and nurtured by this light coming from your heart. See them being healed by it.

5.   Spread that light out further, as far as you can imagine. Comfort someone far away with this warm loving light. Feel the greatness of your heart. Feel the power of your love.

6.   Feel that you are nurturing, healing and comforting all the suffering beings in the world. See them being soothed and loved by the great vast ocean of love within you.

7.   Slowly come back to your own room, to your body. Feel the power of that vast ocean of love that emanated from your chest. Recognize it. Say, "My heart is enormous and guides me to my Brilliantwork."

8.   Answer this question: What work would I love to do that would use my passions and gifts?

9. Recall a time when you passionately pursued something (such as a career or a sport) and you became successful at it. Write the story of what you did.

10. What am I most passionate about right now in my life?
   Write it down.

Ways to Open the Heart

1. Hold a newborn baby in your arms.

2. Visit someone who is dying and listen to them reflect about their life.

3. Call an old friend and apologize.

4. Make a new friend.

5. Climb a mountain.

6. Ask your mother for forgiveness.

7. Ask your father for forgiveness.

8. Forgive your parents.

9. Write a loving letter to someone you've hurt.

10. Drop a grudge you've been carrying.

On My Way to Work

These are the thoughts you should have on your way to work, if the job is right for you:

I can't wait to work on....

I wonder how so and so (an office mate) is doing.

I look forward to that meeting this afternoon.

This is really fun.

I love my job.

If you're not having those thoughts, here are some questions to ask yourself:

What makes me laugh?

When have I been most happy and playful in my life?

In my childhood, what did I love doing?

    Does it offer a clue to my true work?

In my early 20s, what did I love doing?

    Does it offer a clue to my true work?

I'll know I've found my True Work when...

I feel no fear on my first day on the job.

I know effortlessly what to do and how to do it.

Others recognize my natural gifts at this work and praise me for them.

I feel a bit guilty about making money doing this work because it's
    effortless and fun.

My three greatest passions are:

1.

2.

3.

Your Work is Always Serving Someone...

Having purpose and meaning in our work is essential to happiness. We feel useful. We feel our gifts are being used in the world. When I work with clients, I use many different exercises to peel back the layers and help them find their meaningful (and joyful) Brilliantwork. An important step is identifying whom they long to serve with their work.

You can do this by going through a mental checklist of all the different types of people needing your services and picturing yourself working with them. When you imagine working with a certain population you may feel a "yes" in your gut...a stirring of passion. Hold on to that feeling.

For example, when I was a journalist, one of my top values was to educate adults so that they would learn to prevent disease and live long, healthy lives. I wrote for and became editor of publications whose mission was exactly that.

However, the day-to-day reality of my job as magazine editor was a far cry from my longing to help people live healthier lives. I spent my days sitting behind a computer and going to meetings with marketing directors (whose values were usually not in harmony with mine). I finally identified that I needed a career where I actually came face-to-face with the people I was serving. This realization eventually led me to my work as a career counselor.

As I've changed, the people I long to serve have changed as well. This shifting focus has helped guide me to different careers. For example, when I was 19, I was strongly drawn to work with children. That passion led me to my first career as a Montessori teacher. In my role as teacher, I served young children until it was very clear that I needed to work with adults.

However, I still felt drawn to teaching, guiding and inspiring. The population I wanted to focus on had changed, but not my motivation for working. My next careers were working as a career counselor and then as an Outward Bound mountaineering instructor. In both of those roles, I used my talents of teaching, guiding and inspiring. However, I was working with adults – and that population was more fulfilling to me at that point in my life.

You can see how making small changes in your career can enable you to use your innate talents with different populations. If you're currently teaching elementary school and feel strongly that you need a break, perhaps you could become an adult education teacher.

Once you open your mind to new possibilities, you'll be amazed at the options you have. The biggest challenge is letting go of what you know.

This reiterates the importance of working with a career counselor or someone outside of your family and friends who can illuminate new possibilities for you. Do anything you can do to get a fresh perspective on your life. Paying a counselor to talk to you is worthwhile simply because you get a fresh perspective. Answering the open-ended questions that I've sprinkled through this book can give you that fresh viewpoint also. I teach a six-week college course called Finding Work You Love. Again and again, students tell me the most helpful part of the class is the new perspective they gain from my questions and from hearing other people's stories. It empowers them to know they're not alone – that other people share their dreams for joyful work, and that others reinvent themselves even in their fifties. "It's healthy to change direction," said one of my students recently. "I didn't realize that until I took your class."

If we're alive, we're changing. When we have new life experiences, meet new people, enter into new relationships, our values change. Our work needs to reflect these inner changes. This is a key ingredient to finding work you love; understanding that it's okay and even necessary to change.

I've worked with executives who've spent a lifetime in sales. They still love selling but find themselves longing for something different. When we do the "whom will you serve" exercise, they realize they're longing to "serve" a different population. One of my clients had been selling computer software to corporations and was very exhausted from dealing with the challenges of corporate thinking. When he shifted his career to selling health and fitness equipment to health clubs, he felt like he had been "reborn." He loved walking into health clubs and seeing people working hard to get strong and fit. He felt in harmony with the values of health and fitness, and felt deeply connected to the people he was selling equipment to.

I have a friend who is a highly skilled acupuncturist. After years of healing very sick people, he felt depleted and exhausted. He wanted to work with a different population; however he still loved the art of acupuncture. He opened a practice that catered to athletes with sports injuries. He was very gifted at this new work, and he spent his days working with people who were extremely fit and healthy, yet injured from pushing themselves too hard. He felt a deep admiration for this clientele, and his practice became highly successful. He had not given up his innate talent for healing; he had simply changed the population he was healing.

Ask yourself whom you have been serving in your work. Do you feel a deep connection to this population? Are you exhausted from serving them? **Do you still love the work you do, but not the people you serve? It's okay to say "yes" to that. It doesn't mean you're being**

"selfish" or "silly." It simply means you're being honest. That honesty can guide you to joyful work that you'll love. Remember, the only question to ask is: "What do I long to do?"

Again and again in my BrilliantWork program, I ask you to be deeply honest with yourself. This core honesty is essential to finding your Brilliantwork. It will allow you to see past the expectations of others, and past the myths you're carrying around about what you're an expert at, and what your identity is so tightly wrapped up in.

The exercise below will help you clarify whom you're longing to serve. This can be a very helpful clue for finding your BrilliantWork.

Whom Will You Serve?

1. Do I want to work with infants, children, teens, young adults, mid-life adults or seniors?

2. Once I've identified a category, do I want to work with that population when they're healthy, sick, poor, wealthy, gifted, learning disabled, talented, in transition, grieving, successful, afraid, emotionally disturbed, incarcerated, or abused?

3. Can I picture myself serving that population all day long? Does it feel right? Do I feel tense or happy when I think of doing that?

4. Is there a way to serve that population using the same skills I now use in my work? For example, someone who is tired of teaching children can become a teacher of adults – and vice versa.

"To know that even one life has breathed easier because you lived. This is to have succeeded."

Ralph Waldo Emerson

Beth's Story

Beth was a successful career woman in her late 40s. She had worked for large corporations in sales and marketing for more than 20 years. However, she had become very unhappy. During a routine checkup she was diagnosed with a life-threatening disease, and her life went into a tailspin. Lots of soul searching brought her to the conclusion that she needed to change her career to find more joy in her work, which would help her get well.

When I worked with her, the most powerful exercise she did was "Whom will you serve?" In this homework assignment, I asked her to imagine herself working with different populations (such as adults, teens, children, sick people, healthy people, people in transition, etc) until one group really tugged at her heart. She quickly saw that she wanted to work with children. She also identified that she wanted to work with disturbed children. She had a great desire to comfort children.

Everyday she spent 10 minutes dreaming of the future she wanted. She started each morning with the question, "What do I really long to do?" She played the $2 million game and saw herself working for a major organization that offered support and assistance to disturbed children. However, she thought it would be "impossible" to get a job for one of those organizations. So we steadfastly worked on turning around the negative beliefs that would sabotage her efforts. She made a list of 10 positive career affirmations. Whenever she caught herself feeling hopeless about her job search, she turned around her negativity with affirmations.

We imagined her life as perfect as it could be. We saw her with perfect health, two million dollars in the bank, and this wonderful new job. We saw every detail of this new life until she felt it in her cells. She could taste it. She used this vision to pump her energy to the high-end of her continuum. Before sending any correspondence or making any phone calls to the organizations she wanted to work for, she felt the happiness of her new life...**as if she already had it. She basked in this high-end energy every day.**

When she was invited for a job interview, she pumped so much good energy through her body by acting as if she already had the life she wanted...that they offered her the job during the interview.

Today, her life is back on track, her health has improved, and she feels deeply connected with her work.

Past, Present and Future

1. In previous jobs, whom have I served? Give examples. How did that feel?

2. In my present job, whom am I serving? How does that feel?

3. In my future career, whom do I want to serve? How does that feel?

6 Ways to Bring Out Your Best Self

1. Bring a gift to someone who is having a difficult time.

2. Buy groceries for someone who is home sick.

3. Offer a night of free babysitting for a single mom.

4. Write a letter to someone you admire, detailing everything you admire about them.

5. Call a friend and tell them five things you really appreciate about them.

6. Tell a loved one five things you really love about them.

Describe whom you will serve with your work:

I feel best about this part of my life so far:

Now that you've explored your innate talents, passions, dream careers and whom you wish to serve, let's put it all together in an intention statement.

Fill 'Er Up Tip #11: Use Your Intention

One of the most powerful exercises I do with clients is making them write an intention statement for their careers. Your intention statement expresses what you **will** do with your career from a larger perspective, even if you don't yet know the details of exactly what the job will be. It uses the information you've been gathering in all the previous chapters of this book.

Here's one example:

I will use my **unique talents** (to inspire and educate) in order **to serve** (career changers) in a way that is in harmony with my **values** (helping others, independence and creativity).

Your intention statement expresses three things:

1. Your unique talents (gifts) that you bring to the world through your work.

2. Whom you want to serve.

3. Your top three values.

Using the example given above, please write an intention statement using the information you've gathered in previous chapters of this book.

I will use my unique talents

(_____)

in order to serve

(_____)

in a way that is in harmony with my values of

(_____).

Use this intention statement as a guide to the jobs you pursue, the business you start, and the jobs you accept. It becomes a road map guiding you to your true work.

Fill 'er Up Tip #12: Take the Leap!

If we just find another job, any job, it's like taking an aspirin for a headache. We haven't solved the deeper underlying issues that caused the headache in the first place (such as dehydration, eye strain, neck tension, food allergy, etc). Thus the headache (job unhappiness) will probably return.

"There are risks and costs to a program of action. But they are far less than the long-range risks and costs of comfortable inaction."

John F. Kennedy

One of my clients demonstrated this principle recently. She had determined that getting out of new product development for a large corporation and going to work for a non-profit agency was her joyful work. Right before she launched her career in the new direction, a high-paying, prestigious, corporate marketing position was offered to her. She took it. She wanted to give her old career direction another chance – it seemed easier than making a big career change.

Three months later, after slipping into depression and having a minor health scare, she knew that she could no longer do this type of work. Her body was giving her a clear message that she needed a change. She focused her passion on re-launching her career in the new direction, and she was very successful.

I've been called a wholistic career counselor because I focus on the whole person and not just the superficial problem of job unhappiness. I look for the underlying causes of the unhappiness, and I don't just help clients find another job (which is like taking a pain pill without solving the underlying health problem that is causing the pain). I treat the deeper underlying issues of life such as negativity, and I peel back the layers to discover what my clients are really longing for. This is the only way to make real and permanent change. It takes honesty, a little time, and a lot of courage. But the end result is very dramatic.

Here's an example...

Janet's Story

When I first met Janet, she had a bachelor's degree in engineering, had worked briefly and unhappily as an engineer, and was currently a pension plan manager at a large corporation.

This creative, funny, high-spirited woman (brilliant enough to belong to MENSA) was drowning in bureaucracy, meaningless day-to-day tasks, and micro-management. Because of her genius-level IQ, she had been pushed into one inappropriate field after another. She had become so depressed that her doctor prescribed anti-depressants, which she took daily. One night while surfing the web, she came across my BrilliantWork website.

Immediately, Janet called me, and I began helping her identify and find joyful work that she would love doing and that would be in harmony with her innate values and talents. We started with her dreams. After weeks of asking herself, "What do I really want?" she saw that working at a University would be a perfect fit for her. She loved working with college students and being on campus. She longed to get another degree. She also recognized that her brilliant mind was sometimes her worst enemy – since she often focused on negative beliefs and outcomes. We worked relentlessly on turning around her negative thoughts with positive affirmations. She created a daily "energy" plan that included dreaming, exercise, laughter and positive affirmations.

We imagined a full bank account, perfect health, lots of joy, and a university job that she loved. She saw it and felt it until it made her giddy.

She started each day with that vision and that feeling. From there, she did informational interviews, made phone calls and did networking, but only when her vibrations were as high as she could get them with her dreams.

Two months later, Janet found a job at a local college working as an outplacement specialist and enrolled in the school's Master's in Counseling program. The most amazing result was her happiness. She woke up happy in the morning, and her day-to-day activities felt deeply joyful to her and in harmony with her values. She also enjoyed the evening graduate course-work that was leading her in a direction she felt passionate about.

Looking Deeply Beyond the Surface...

When I look back at what got me into trouble with my previous career, it was my inability to stop, take a deep breath, and see that I had changed, and that my career needed to change. When I was finally ready to change, I saw a career counselor and these were the types of questions we worked with. These questions changed my life – for the better. As you've completed each assignment in this program, you've already answered these 11 questions. Now it's time to put them together. Spend some time with these questions; you've nearly reached your pot of gold.

11 Ways to Get to the Core of the Problem

1. What are my three top values and are they in harmony with my current work?

2. Whom do I want to serve? Am I serving them in my current work?

3. What are my three greatest innate gifts or talents? Am I using these in my current career?

4. What insights into my patterns and potential do my friends give me?

5. What insights into my potential does my current job give me?

6. What is my greatest passion?

7. What am I here on this earth to do?

8. What career do I see myself doing happily for the next five years?

9. How can I be more graceful in my life and my work?

10. What is my dream career and what does it teach me?

11. What do I really want in my life?

Ten Ways to Identify Your BrilliantWork

1. When you imagine yourself doing this work day after day, you smile automatically.

2. When you think of explaining this as your life's work (at the end of your life), you feel content and satisfied.

3. The idea of doing this work seems "fun" to you, therefore you wonder if it could really be "work."

4. This work will come naturally to you, allowing you to bring your best self to meet the world.

5. This work will bring the parts of yourself that you most enjoy to blossom.

6. You can't imagine you'd be so lucky as to be "allowed" to do this for a living.

7. As you settle into this work, you feel blessed and happy so that your interactions with others are kinder and gentler.

8. You begin to understand that everything (painful and wonderful) that has happened to you in this life has brought you to this place to be able to do this work for the world.

9. You're eager to go to work in the morning.

10. You feel good about modeling this work to your children as an example of joyful work.

Write your thoughts about the list above.

Are you experiencing any of these reactions to the jobs / careers you're considering right now?

REMEMBER THE
GREAT COSMIC JOKE:

*If you want to find
your BrilliantWork,
act and feel as if
you already have it.*

*That joy and passion
will then attract the
perfect work to you.*

Chapter Four

Use Your Energy

to move through pain and fear.

Consider the possibility that all of your pain, (every wound you've experienced from loss to illness to disappointment) was exactly what you needed (and chose) in order to arrive at this point in your life.

It's all perfect! All the pain, loss, despair, illness and struggle was for a purpose and you chose it.

Why do we experience pain? It moves us forward, wakes us up and gives us wisdom and compassion. It's impossible to have a lifetime without experiencing pain. It's the human experience. However, we do have a choice in the matter.

Our choice is how we react to the pain and what we choose to learn from it.

This is where our energy work comes in. Remember your energy continuum and how we compared it to a fuel tank? When your energy tank is full, you feel connected to everything good – from divinity to inspiration, love, joy, optimism and strength. When your tank is low, you're lost in anger, despair, pessimism and fear. You're separated from your true self and your ability to move forward. When faced with a life challenge such as losing someone you love, doesn't it serve you to have a full energy tank? If your energy tank is full when disaster hits, you can plow through the crisis with clarity and force. You won't get lost in the pain.

"There is no coming to consciousness without pain." Carl Jung

You WILL have pain in your life. But you will recover more quickly, move forward in a more positive direction and easily attract new people and circumstances into your life when your energy tank is full.

Now we're back to our original discussion of how we fill our energy tank each day? How do we keep our energy at the high-end of our continuum when we experience pain? And how can we quickly learn what we need to learn from the pain and move on?

EPR Moves You Through Pain!

Don't forget EPR! These three quick energy shifts you learned in Chapter One that I call EPR will pull you smoothly through any crisis. Remember? **They're Sweetness, Humor and Gratitude.**

Step One

When feeling pain, **humor** is a quick way to shift out of pain into a realization of the bigger picture of why you're here. It helps you understand that your pain is but a small blip in the big picture of your life. Laugh at yourself, and laugh with the person you believe is making you feel pain. Laughter will quickly raise you above and beyond the pain. It will enlighten your perspective and shed light into your darkness.

Step Two

Find your childlike innocence (**sweetness**) when you're feeling pain. Accessing your innate sweetness will allow you to ask for help. Sweetness is our divine right. When we show anyone (even God) our sweetness, we receive assistance immediately. As you get in touch with your sweetness, ASK God, the higher beings, or the deities (whomever you believe in) to come and guide you through the pain and into the light.

We are never alone. At this moment, there are divine beings trying to guide you. When you ask to be pulled into the light, you will feel loved instantly. Use prayer, meditation, chanting or singing to call for guidance. You're not on this journey alone – no matter how much it feels that way. In your darkest moments, ask for guidance, and you will receive it.

If you only believe in physics and energy, look at it this way. The quantum physicists know that everything is energy, and all this energy comes from a source of energy we call Source Energy. This source energy is also your source. To get this source energy to help you, you must align yourself with its high-end vibrations. Once you're aligned with this high energy, you're in the "flow" of life and living life to its highest potential. Therefore, your challenge is the same, whether you believe in physics or spirituality. You must raise your energy levels and align them with source energy so that you can access goodness and inspiration. This will move you through your pain.

Step Three

As hard as this may seem, feel **gratitude** for your pain. The pain is teaching you something important. There's an important connection between your pain and your work. Ask yourself, "What is the greatest pain that I feel right now?" Let yourself feel it, then ask for understanding about this pain. Ask to be shown the purpose of your pain so that you can release it.

From working with thousands of clients and studying the life stories of hundreds of people, **I am 100% SURE that our pain guides us to our BrilliantWork.** I have many examples I'll share with you later in this chapter. Consider the possibility that you chose (consciously or unconsciously) every important job you've had in your lifetime because it was healing you. What pain needs healing now? Let that answer guide you to your BrilliantWork.

Our work heals us by letting us offer to the world exactly what we need to heal ourselves.

I'll give you an example from my life. In my 20s I enjoyed a career as a mountaineering instructor for Colorado Outward Bound School. I loved empowering people and inspiring them to overcome their fears. My own childhood had been filled with fear and feeling unempowered. This work of empowering others felt very meaningful to me; it was healing my wounds. And I was having great fun!

I was happily married to a fellow mountaineer and we had a good life filled with rock climbing adventures and mountaineering trips. My husband, Paul, had stomach problems for awhile but was told by a couple doctors that it was nothing more than a nervous stomach or the beginnings of an ulcer. By the time we got a proper diagnosis of colon cancer, the doctors gave him two weeks to live. (This was in the late 70s before colonoscopies were used routinely.)

Paul died one year later. From that moment on, I couldn't climb or teach mountaineering anymore. My life changed, and my work changed. I went back to school to study journalism and spent the next 15 years of my life working as a newspaper reporter (health writer), magazine editor (writing about natural health), and a VP of Content for natural health websites. I was passionate about writing stories that helped people prevent disease and live long, healthy lives. I was healing my own pain with each story I wrote. When the pain was finally put to rest, I felt drawn back to my work of empowering and inspiring others. That desire brought me to career counseling.

As I look back, I can see 30 years later, that it was a nearly overwhelming experience going through Paul's death with him. I believe that I made a "soul agreement" to go through that terrible trauma for a reason. It forced me so deeply into my pessimism and cynicism that I was finally forced to break free of my negativity. It brought my darkness (fear, sadness and anger) so clearly to the surface, that I could see my dark side for what it was. Only then could I make a positive choice to change it. An easier life wouldn't have revealed my negativity to me so clearly.

When you find yourself in extremely challenging circumstances, ask yourself why you chose it. Ask yourself what you're supposed to be changing. Ask for divine guidance.

"Often I have found that the one thing that can save is the thing which appears most to threaten ...One has to go down into what one most fears and in that process comes a saving flicker of light and energy that, even if it does not produce the courage of a hero, at any rate enables a trembling mortal to take one step further."

Laurens Van Der Post

Fill 'er Up Tip #13: Use your deepest pain as fuel to find your BrilliantWork.

Margaret's Story

Margaret was a very successful journalist with a thriving career as magazine editor and author. At the age of 40, she came to me for career counseling. As successful as her career had been, she was no longer happy with it.

We took a look at her deeper issues, and she revealed that until recently she had denied a deep childhood trauma from sexual abuse. By recognizing it and getting therapy from a child-abuse expert, she was beginning to heal.

This healing process had gotten her in touch with a strong desire to do meaningful work in the world. She wanted to become a therapist for adult survivors of child abuse, or she wanted to write about these survivors whom she felt so deeply connected to.

First she had to recognize how her "victim energy" was affecting her life. By giving Margaret energy experiments to do each day, she gradually realized she was making her pain worse with her negative thoughts and beliefs. This made it important to her to learn to use her energy to make things better rather than worse.

She worked daily to boost her energy to the higher end of her continuum – in spite of her pain. By focusing on friendships, laughter and gratitude, she made a major energy shift to happiness. As she shifted, so did the events in her life. New people and opportunities came pouring in. She experienced joy for the first time in years.

By going through the BrilliantWork exercises and career questions, she identified a desire to do volunteer work with women survivors of abuse. She wanted to have day-to-day contact with people in a way that tangibly helped them – rather than sitting behind a computer all day. To meet this need, she volunteered two days a week at a local organization for victims of sexual abuse. We worked relentlessly on turning around her negative thoughts and beliefs. Her daily affirmation became:

I intend to move forward with my life and not focus on my pain. I intend to find work that heals my pain and brings me joy.

Margaret quickly bonded with the women she was helping. As they shared their life stories with her, she was inspired to write them down. Soon, she was writing magazine articles and a book proposal based on the lives of these women. Today, she continues writing and volunteering. These two activities combined give her joy and a sense of purpose. She is, once again, very inspired and passionate about her career.

Sharon's Story

Sharon had a powerful career as a publisher. After 20 successful years, her work was not satisfying her anymore. Because she was extremely bright, she was confident that she "could" do a number of different types of careers and be successful at them. This thought process exhausted her and thwarted her efforts at moving forward in a new direction. At our first session, I asked her, **"What do you really want?"**

"I'm not used to answering that question," she explained. "I've always asked myself what should I do or what is the right thing to do, but not what do I want to do."

As we let that question sit on the backburner of her subconscious, we focused on identifying her greatest source of pain as a clue to her direction. She revealed that her greatest childhood pain had been one of feeling rejected by her peers during adolescence – when acceptance was very important to her.

Through understanding how this pain had affected her, she recognized a need to help other people feel accepted and respected by their peers. By completing the BrilliantWork career exercises, and by answering my initial question "What do you really want?" she found her direction. Being an Executive Coach helping high-powered business people improve their social skills and thus gain more acceptance and respect from their peers was her BrilliantWork. She took some training to do that, launched her own business, and today has a thriving practice as an executive coach.

She spends her days working with high-powered and successful clients who are very good at certain skills (such as sales and marketing), yet have great trouble managing people because of poor social skills.

Sharon uses tremendous compassion and insight to help these people "soften their edges" and become kinder, gentler executives. With each client she helps, she feels a piece of her childhood wound disappearing.

Jim's Story

Many of my male clients tell me they don't feel any pain and have led very happy lives. From years of experience, I've learned that these men frame their pain differently than women do. They use different words to describe pain, and it takes awhile to identify it. But once it's revealed, they get enormous clarity of direction.

For example, Jim was a high-powered Fortune 500 executive who had lived a very "perfect" life. He came to me because he was searching for a new, more meaningful career direction. I gave him a BrilliantWork home-work assignment called "When I was a child." In this assignment he was to write about his childhood memories and explain his greatest childhood challenges. I was greatly inspired by his story: At a young age, he had been diagnosed with a life-threatening disease and was told he would never walk again. He spent two years in a hospital bed unable to move.

Eventually, he recovered and proved the doctors wrong. From that moment on, his life was filled with amazing athletic accomplishments and career successes. In his BrilliantWork notebook he wrote: "They told me I would never walk again. I became determined to run through life and never look back. I over-achieved at everything. I never asked "why?" or reflected on the meaning of life. I couldn't keep still that long...until I hit a wall of emptiness in my personal life."

Clearly, Jim's deepest pain had been his fear of being unable to "move forward" with his life. Now as he examined that pain, he realized it was time to slow down and stop chasing after accomplishments. It was time to reflect on who he was, what his gifts were, and how he could serve others.

He identified that much of his success came because he was running away from something – not towards something. From our discussions of the energy continuum, he realized this behavior was functioning from the lower end of his continuum; he was motivating himself through fear. Now he wanted to be motivated by passion and compassion – rather than fear. He believed this would lead him to happiness and inner peace.

His pain became his guide to having deeper, more meaningful relationships with his loved ones, as well as finding kinder, gentler work that served the world. Today, he teaches at a major University where he loves teaching college graduate students how to succeed in the business world.

Bruce's Story

Bruce was a miserable computer programmer in his 40s. His only joy was race-car driving, which he spent his weekends doing. His marriage was in trouble, and he was taking anti-depressants. His doctor sent him to see me, because Bruce was so unhappy with his career.

When I asked Bruce what he really wanted, he replied that he had never asked himself that question in his entire life. So I began by focusing on his buried pain. He completed the same BrilliantWork homework assignment that I described above. Bruce's story was unforgettable:

When Bruce was 13, his older sister woke him up one night. "Get up! Mom and dad have gone out. Get in the back seat of the car and shut up," she whispered. "Don't ever tell them about this."

His sister had just gotten her driver's license. She told Bruce she was going to see how fast the car would go around the curves in their neighborhood. Bruce agreed to go with his sister. He fell asleep in the back seat and only remembers waking up in the darkness, in a ditch, unable to find his sister. She was pinned under the car and died instantly. That moment changed his life forever. His parents divorced, his father became an alcoholic, and "no one ever spoke about the accident. In fact, no one ever spoke at all," he remembered. Bruce became an outcast in high school and learned to bottle up his feelings. "Have a stiff upper lip and carry on," was his father's only advice.

As we explored this memory together, Bruce realized that each time he raced a car at 80 miles an hour around a race track he was healing a childhood wound. He was reliving and re-programming the event that had destroyed his childhood. He was taking control of his greatest pain – the loss of his sister and family.

By understanding his pain, Bruce gave himself permission to pursue a career as a race car driving instructor and a race car service and repair shop owner. By honestly sharing his new insights with his wife and daughter, he rallied their support for his new career. He found new intimacy in his marriage, and he gave himself permission to have a career that he loved.

Today he is much happier and healthier. He says that each time he teaches someone to master speeding around a race track at 80 mph, he heals a deep wound in himself. He believes his work is meaningful and it makes him happy. He has found his BrilliantWork.

Here's the secret:

The more pain you feel,
the more energy you have to launch
your new career.
See the pain as fuel —
not as something that stops you
from moving forward.

Using My Pain to Guide Me

Here are a few questions to ask yourself to help uncover the wound that is calling out to be healed. Write your answers down.

1. When I think about all the people in the world who need help, I am most drawn to help... (identify specifically...children who are abused, grieving adults, hungry children...etc.)

2. What I most want to do for these people is to: (be specific – some people might say organize a foundation to provide services and money to them, while others would say to love and hold them. Each answer is another clue to the exact type of work you're drawn to do.)

3. When I was a child, what caused me the greatest pain and why? (Go into detail as much as you can.)

4. In my entire life, what caused me the most pain and why?

5. When I look at my answers to these questions, I gain these insights:

The next exercise is a powerful way to identify your personal pain and use it as a guide to uncovering your "true work."

A Guided Meditation For Recognizing & Releasing Your Deepest Pain

1. Get comfortable. Lean back against something, but don't let your head rest on anything. Hold your head erect. If you lean your head back, you are more likely to fall asleep during your meditation. By keeping it upright, you'll wake yourself up if your head starts to slump over as you fall asleep. Let your hands rest peacefully in your lap. Close your eyes.

2. Take a deep breath and follow that breath as it goes down into your lungs. Imagine it going down into your belly as you expand your stomach. Pull in your stomach and feel the breath coming up your chest and out through your nostrils. Do this breathing pattern slowly and with awareness five times.

3. Let your breathing become more normal and find its own relaxed rhythm.

4. Ask yourself quietly, **"What image from my life makes me feel like crying when I think about it?"**

5. Your strongest pain will usually reveal itself almost instantly when you ask that question. You'll get a visual image of the experience that hurt you so much. Stay with the vision and **let your heart feel that pain** – really experience it – recognize it. Cry it out if that feels good to you. Honor and recognize that pain. Don't run from it. Give it a few minutes of your attention.

6. When you have stayed with that pain for several moments (no longer than five minutes), you've truly felt it and recognized it, **then hold your hands in front of your chest with the palms facing up.** Take several slow, deep breaths. Imagine putting that pain into your open palms. **See the pain coming out of your chest and into your hands.**

7. Raise your hands towards heaven and **offer that pain up and away from you.** Set it free. If you believe in God, offer it to God. If you believe in Buddha, offer it to Buddha. If you believe in physics, offer it to the Source Energy. Move it out of your chest and away from you.

8. Put your hands back into your lap in a relaxed position. Take five more slow, deep breaths visualizing the breath moving down to expand your belly and then up and out through your nostrils.

9. Say a prayer of gratitude. Tell God you're grateful for your life and want to know your purpose here.

10. Slowly come back to awareness of the room around you. Open your eyes. Sit still for a few minutes breathing deeply.

11. This particular type of meditation is used by people who are **recovering from grief.** By feeling the pain once a day, truly experiencing it and then releasing it, many people find that the pain quits gnawing at them for the remainder of the day. It's as if you've made an appointment

to feel that pain, honor it, release it, and then get on with your day. If you sense that this practice could help you recover from a loss, do it once a day.

12. Make a list of the careers you've had and ask yourself what pain you were healing with each job. Ask, "What new career would best heal this pain I'm feeling now?" Write down any answers that come to you.

The Three Best Antidotes to Pain

Laughter shows you the bigger perspective of life and minimizes your personal drama. It brings you to another dimension where inner healing can take place.

Love opens the heart allowing us to feel our pain and thus move through it to greater love and happiness. It moves your energy to the high end of your continuum.

Compassion forgives the source of your pain and allows you to move forward with love and courage.

Putting Them to Work for You

1. Write down your three favorite **comedies** and plan to watch one a week for three weeks.

2. Write down the three **people who make you laugh** the most and plan to spend an hour with one of them each week for three weeks.

3. Write down three **people you love dearly** and plan to visit one of them each week for three weeks.

4. **Write a letter** to three people you haven't communicated with in a long time.

5. Write the names of three people you haven't forgiven. **Pray** to find the compassion to forgive them.

One insight I have about my emotional pain is this:

My pain leads me to this realization about my meaningful work:

By facing your pain,
you turn it into energy.
It becomes your ally, and
it moves you forward.

Chapter Five

See It!

Always script the future you want – before taking action.

"Nothing happens unless first a dream."
Carl Sandburg

When we dream and imagine what we want to happen, we tap into source energy. We tap into the boundless realm of ever-changing possibilities – rather than our limited view of fixed outcomes which is all we can see from the bottom end of our continuum.

By changing our negative beliefs about what is possible, and instead seeing positive outcomes to our challenges, we set the energy in place to make what we want to happen. This is called scripting.

Before going to the job interview that "you know you won't get" or before asking a banker (or relative) for a new business loan, take a moment and see the interaction going beautifully with everyone operating from their high-end (especially you). See the banker saying, "Yes, I think we can put something together to help you launch your business." See the company CEO saying, "We're always looking for people like you. When can you start?" See lots of laughter and good feeling in the room. Feel how happy you'll be after the meeting.

Consider the possibility that if you spent even a couple minutes each day seeing positive outcomes for all of your "worries"– your life would go in a better direction. Isn't it worth a little experimenting?

Consider how much time you currently spend imagining worse-case scenarios. Realize that each second you spend imagining those scenarios you are actually attracting negative energy into your life?

Like attracts like...

If you really understood how powerful you are and how you create your "reality" with your thoughts, dreams and beliefs – your life would instantly improve. By not accepting responsibility for the effect your energy has on the circumstances of your life – you remain a victim. Victims hate their jobs, can't find better ones, can't launch their own businesses, are often sick, and seldom have enough money. Are you a victim?

First ask, "What do I really want?" Then see it happening. Those two steps are enough to change your life dramatically.

Victims suffer from poor health. Why? Because our health is, of course, linked to our thoughts and beliefs...

The Energy of Health

The same energetic principles that apply to finding work you love also apply to finding perfect health. Have you ever had a stress headache or an upset stomach caused by anxiety? Those health problems are obvious results of negative thoughts and beliefs. But how about heart disease, cancer, and the millions of other illnesses we struggle with?

Scientific research supports the notion that our happiness (our energy) is directly connected to our health. Dean Ornish, M.D., author of *Love & Survival*, found that heart attack patients recovered much quicker when they felt loved and nurtured by someone in their community. He also found that the incidence of heart disease was lower in communities where there was a strong sense of connection and caring (high-end emotions).

Candace Pert, Ph.D., author of *Molecules of Emotion*, researched neuropeptides and found that these molecules provide a scientifically proven link between mind and body. In other words, she says, there's scientific proof that our thoughts and emotions affect our health – for better and for worse.

This explains why we need to ask ourselves, "What do I really want?"

If we're not living the life we really want, we're not going to function from the high end of our continuum. We'll be spending too much time immersed in our negative emotions of depression, pessimism, anger and anxiety. Marinating in those negative emotions will cause illnesses. Our only pathway back to health will be to head in the direction of the life we really want.

We must see a good life, perfect health, and fulfilling careers. These dreams will open doors for us. We'll move forward in a positive direction. We'll find ourselves living from the higher end of our continuum – marinating in positive emotions of love, joy, optimism and peacefulness. Good health will return.

Take a moment to write three negative beliefs you have about your health. For example, my father died from heart disease so I probably will too. Or, I have so much stress in my life that I'm sure I'll get an ulcer. Or, the chances are one-in-three that I'll get some kind of cancer.

Write positive antidotes to those negative beliefs. For example: I intend to take good care of myself and live a long, healthy life. Or, I'm tapped into the source of energy and good health. Nothing can make me sick when I tap into source energy. Or, my cells are in perfect alignment with good health when I go to the high-end of my continuum because that's where divine order exists. I am basking in perfect health (divine order) whenever I feel positive emotions.

The journey to perfect health begins with your thoughts and beliefs. You must believe you can have perfect health, you must see yourself as perfectly healthy, and you must live the life you really want...or begin to go in the direction of the life you really want. Just taking the first step forward puts you in alignment with source energy and perfect health. See it and you can have it!

> "Go confidently in the direction of your dreams! Live the life you've imagined."
>
> *Henry David Thoreau*

Michael's Story

Michael's father and brother both died from heart attacks at the age of 56. Michael was 49 when he came to see me. "My father and brother were workaholics and the stress killed them. I've been living my life the same way they did. I need to make a big change in my career direction," he said during our first session.

I asked Michael to write down some beliefs about work that he had learned from his family. He gave me a list of ten very negative beliefs that had been handed down through generations of his family members. These included: "Life is very hard. If you don't work hard, you don't get anywhere." "Only selfish, spoiled people have easy lives." "Only women watch what they eat and take care of their health." "There's nothing you can do to prevent heart disease in our family, so you might as well not bother."

Michael wrote positive antidotes next to each of these negative beliefs. These included: "When I tap into my positive emotions of love, happiness and contentment, I experience perfect health. I intend to marinate in my positive emotions everyday. I intend to live a long, happy, healthy life."

I asked what his life would look like if he had the life he really wanted. After a few days of contemplating this question, he wrote, "I would become the wood worker I always wanted to be – and not the stockbroker I always thought I had to be."

He pictured a life working from home in his garage – building custom high-end furniture (which he had a proven talent for). He saw himself exercising daily, eating good food and living a long healthy life. From that moment on, he was inspired by his dream.

He worked everyday to keep his energy on the higher end of his continuum. He was vigilant with his thoughts and beliefs. Within a very short time, he had reinvented his life and created the life he had dreamed of. Five years later, Michael has perfect health and work that he loves.

The Energy of Money

Consider the possibility that (as the physicists say) money is energy too. And consider the possibility that the only thing stopping you from having financial ease and abundance is your negative thinking. Can you imagine yourself wealthy and living a life of ease? Can you picture it?

That's the first step – believing you can have it and seeing your life with it.

I've worked with hundreds of clients who say, "I hate my job and I only stay with it to pay the bills." I ask if they've created financial ease with this job they hate so much. The answer is always no. They're hardly making ends meet – no matter how big their salary is. Why? Because money doesn't flow to us when we're stuck in our negative energy. It's impossible for the energy of money to flow through our negativity.

Only by following your high-end emotions to find work you love will you create true financial abundance in your life. If you stay at a job you hate, you might make a reasonable salary and have some savings. But the money will disappear like water running through your fingers – unless you are living and working from the high-end of your continuum.

When you're doing work you love, feeling empowered and inspired, the money follows. When you hate your work, it hates you back. Like attracts like. Find your Brilliantwork and love your life. It's the only recipe for true wealth.

Spend some time reading biographies of wealthy people like Oprah and Donald Trump. The most successful people all say the same thing:

Find your passion and follow it – no matter what. Never give up. Believe you can do it. Believe you can be rich. See it and you can have it.

"Happiness depends on ourselves."

Aristotle

Remember the story of two New York entrepreneurs who started a very successful nightclub in the 70s? These two guys were the kings of Manhattan for many years. Everyone wanted to get into their nightclub; it was THE place to go for celebrities as well as everyday people. Each night, a huge line of people would form outside the door. The owners would walk down the line and hand-pick the select few who were allowed to enter.

After becoming millionaires, these two owners were arrested and went to jail for tax evasion and drug dealing. They spent several years in jail, went bankrupt and lost all of their famous friends. When they got out of jail, they came up with a new business idea. They wrote a business plan, got it funded, and today they're millionaires again. Their new business is restoring old Manhattan hotels.

It was their refusal to believe that they were "not worthy" of being wealthy that turned them into millionaires for a second time. Instead they focused on solutions and asked "What do I really want? "When they saw their new dream, they went after it passionately. They believed they would be successful again. They believed they would be wealthy again. And so they were.

Write down three of your negative thoughts about money. For example: "No matter how hard I work, I never get ahead."; "The economy is so bad that it's impossible to make good money."; "Everything is so expensive these days; I'll never be able to buy a house."

Write three positive antidotes next to each of these negative beliefs. For example: "I intend to find work I love that brings me financial abundance."; "I intend to work from the high-end of my continuum, and my work will be recognized and rewarded."; "The universe is abundant, and there is no lack of anything. When I'm in the high-end of my continuum, I tap into boundless abundance."

Fill 'er Up Tip #14: See the future you really want and believe it is possible. Only then can you have it!

Seeing the Connections

1. If I died tomorrow, would I die as a happy person?

2. If not, what three steps can I take to begin changing that right now?

3. Do I believe there's a link between my health and my happiness?

4. If so, how can I get happier?

5. Do I believe there's a link between my job and my happiness?

6. If so, how can I find a career that makes me happier?

7. Did either of my parents die early deaths due to health problems that I may be able to prevent? How so? What am I willing to do about it?

Write down your thoughts about your relationship with money and how you could improve it.

If I died tomorrow, what would I most regret?

What can I do today to turn that regret into something I'm proud of?

"In the depth of winter, I finally learned that there was in me an invincible summer."

Albert Camus

When I think of this quote, I'm reminded of my most miserable job. A company I had worked for as VP of Content was sold to another company, and suddenly I found myself working for a corporation that didn't want me, didn't like me, cut my salary by twenty percent, and didn't allow me to oversee content the way I had done for 15 years. I went from having work I loved, a great salary, and lots of recognition to sitting in a cubicle writing an annual report for a company that I didn't believe in.

Why was I sitting in that cubicle being miserable? Because I was afraid. I fell into my negativity. I couldn't find a better job, and I was afraid of walking away, losing my income, losing my home, and ruining my daughter's life.

Instead, I ruined my life anyway. I cried every night. I was deeply depressed, and couldn't sleep. I was getting sick every other week. My daughter was missing a tremendous amount of school because of made-up illnesses that disappeared once we got home. (She was doing her part to get me out of that cubicle).

In my fear of ruining my daughter's life, I was ruining her life anyway. And because I hated my job, it hated me back. For the first time in my life, I was fired. It was humiliating and painful and a loud wake-up call. But getting out of that cubicle helped me get clarity about what I was doing wrong *(thinking negatively)* and how to change it *(focus on solutions)*.

Later, when I made the career/life change that brought me to career counseling, the change in our happiness was immense and took place nearly overnight. Today my business is successful, and I have a life I only dreamed was possible. The seeds of this new life were born in my misery.

If you find yourself in Albert Camus' "depth of winter," you need to change directions. You're being forced to the edge of your misery so that you will change. How far will you allow yourself to go into your negativity? After I started BrilliantWork.com and began doing the work I loved, my entire demeanor changed. I interacted with people in a new, easy way. I was smiling much more and looked 10 years younger.

Everywhere I went, people commented on how wonderful I looked and how happy I seemed. I hadn't changed my physical appearance in any way, yet I was "in the groove" of my life – doing the work I was meant to do. People asked me if I was in love. Yes, I was in love with my work.

Enlightenment is easy with hindsight. The trick is figuring out what's wrong when you're in the middle of the problem. I was blinded by my fears. I was not focusing on solutions. I was stuck in the low-end of my energy continuum. I saw myself as a victim of the bad economy.

Perhaps you've been blinded by your fears of financial disaster. Lift the veil of fear and move to the other side. It's like turning on a light in a dark room. Ask yourself, "What do I really want?" Dream of your perfect life. See it. Feel it. Believe it. The rest will fall into place.

When you're doing work you love, you function from the high-end of your continuum, and the money follows. Your passion, happiness and joy will open doors you never thought possible. As the poet *Robert Bly* says, "Follow your bliss..."

Are You in Your Depth of Winter?

1. Am I arguing with people at work over small things?

2. Do I sabotage things at work? (A client of mine wrote an email to her best friend complaining about her boss, but accidently sent the email to her boss.)

3. Am I tossing and turning most of the night?

4. Is my health falling apart?

5. Do I feel like my life is going nowhere?

6. Do I cry easily?

7. Do I remember times in my life when I felt inspired and happy?

If you answered yes to those questions, you are in your "depth of Winter." Now, dream of a better life.

Believe it and you can have it.

6 Ways to Get in the Groove

1.   Shut your Daytimer for one week.

2.   Turn off your computer for one week.

3.   Dream of a better life.

4.   Pump your energy to the high-end in spite of circumstances.

5.   Ask "What do I really want?"

6.   Find work you love.

What is the Groove?

1.   Recall a time when you felt like you were living "in the moment" and didn't feel stressed or anxious.

2.   Describe the details of that time. Describe what that sense of ease was like for you.

3.   Do you ever feel that sense of ease now in your life? When?

4.   What is one thing you can do to feel that ease in your life today?

Describe the last time you felt you were "following your bliss." What were you doing? How did it feel?

Write down three things you can do this week to follow your bliss.

Am I in my "depth of winter?"

What can I do to get back in the groove?

Here's an evaluation technique that helps you **SEE and FEEL** a new career before moving forward with it:

A Day In the Life

Select a career that you have often considered pursuing. Go through the following exercise in order to get a clear answer about whether or not you should pursue it.

1. Close your eyes, take a deep breath, and get comfortable. Eliminate all background noise. Sit quietly and still for one minute before moving on to the next step in this exercise. (It's helpful to do the centering exercise before visualizing your day in the life of a new career.)

2. Imagine you have this new career (the one you've often considered pursuing). **Picture yourself waking up in the morning getting ready for work.** See yourself getting dressed, getting in the car to drive to work. Picture yourself arriving at the office. Picture your desk.

3. **Notice how your body feels while you visualize this day.** How does your throat feel? Restricted or relaxed? How does your stomach feel? How does your chest feel?

4. See yourself going through the workday. Visualize the people you work with; how old they are, how they interact with you, what your relationships are like. **Picture yourself doing the exact tasks** required in this new job – all day long.

5. Picture yourself coming home from work at the end of the day. You greet your family as you return home. **What do you tell them about your day?** How do you feel? Check in with your body? With your throat, chest and stomach.

6. Do you feel renewed, excited, refreshed? How does your stomach feel? Is there tension in your body as you imagine this new career? Do you feel excited and happy, or depressed and drained when you think of spending a day at this work? How do you describe this workday to your friends?

7. Write down all of your **physical experiences** as you went through this visualization. Did you get a strong "yes" or "no" about pursuing this career?

When I visualize a day in the life of a career (from my list of careers I've often thought of doing), I get a "yes" response to these careers:

My greatest insight from visualizing a day in the life of different careers is this:

Chapter Six

Take Action

Research, network, and interview – only while operating from the high-end of your continuum.

"The unexamined life is not worth living."
Plato

After doing the inner explorations described in previous chapters, it's essential to take action. Go out into the world and research your new ideas. Meet people, network, make phone calls, hand out your resume and business cards; take tangible action steps in a new direction.

Why? It's a law of physics; once an object begins moving forward it takes on a force (energy) of its own. Once YOU move forward in any direction – even the wrong direction – you'll be pulled into the flow of forward-moving energy, and you'll be guided to the right people and opportunities. You'll become part of a vortex of positive energy that moves you into the right place at the right time; forward action takes on a life of its own.

Inaction, sitting at home worrying or being unhappy, will not open any doors. You MUST take a step forward in your new direction – then doors will open. The students who take my workshops and classes tell me this is often the most helpful thing about my class. Everyone must promise the group three things they'll do in a week to research their new career direction. When class meets again, everyone reports on their actions and the results. It's inspiring to hear 30 people report on the small action steps they took (such as making phone calls or meeting with someone) because those small steps ALWAYS produce results. They lead to another meeting or another phone call. My students look better, sound better, and FEEL better than they did when they were stagnating – not taking action.

FEELING better is the most important step you can ever take. Remember your fuel tank? You're filling up your energy tank every time you do anything that makes you feel better. The fuller your tank, the better your life will get. Good energy attracts good circumstances.

"But I'm still not sure which direction to go in," you say.

That doesn't matter a hoot, I say. (Because you actually DO know.)

Remember your list of "careers you keep considering" from chapter two? You went through that list visualizing a day in the life of each possible career. You got positive gut feeling responses from 2 or 3 of those possible careers. Look at your top three possibilities and decide which career excites you the most. The one that makes you giggle is the first one you should pursue. Take at least three steps in the direction of that career. If nothing opens up after two weeks, take three steps in the direction of your second choice. It's that simple. You're going to follow the good energy – wherever it takes you.

FIRST...Remember that you are ENERGY and everything around you is made of ENERGY.

This is an interactive universe, according the physicists. Therefore the results of your action steps depend on your energy! In other words, the more positive high-end energy – happiness, optimism, divinity and inspiration you can pump through your body before making any phone calls or going to any meetings – the better the outcomes will be. GUARANTEED!

Pump your energy by dreaming of the life you want, imagining you already have it, asking for divine guidance, exercising, meditating and sending out love and positive energy to everyone you interact with. Before making any phone calls, stand up, walk around, laugh out loud, and smile while you make the call. Before going to any meetings, put on an outfit that makes you happy, go for a 30 minute daydreaming walk, and call someone who makes you laugh.

ALWAYS script meetings first by seeing them happening the way you want them to. Picture all meetings and phone calls ending with good feelings all around and new possibilities being discussed.

Write down the best possible outcomes you'd like to see happen. Picture that desired outcome and feel the good energy you'll be feeling when you walk out of the meeting. Hear the words you want to hear. See smiles and warm handshakes all around.

These are things that <u>WON'T</u> help you:

Endlessly complaining about your unhappiness; watching television, worrying, being angry or afraid, giving up, getting drunk, taking drugs.

These are things that <u>WILL</u> help you:

Pumping your energy to the high-end of your continuum, dreaming of what you want, laughing, seeing a coach / counselor / therapist who makes you move forward, asking for divine guidance, meditating, taking three action steps in ANY new career direction.

Howard's Story

Howard had his own business teaching foreign languages. He loved his work, yet the economy had gotten bad and his business was very slow. With a wife and three kids to support and bills piling up, his marriage was in trouble, and he was extremely depressed. Everyone told him to just get a job – any job – to support his family. The thought of giving up the work he loved devastated him. Yet the thought of losing his family was devastating also. He felt trapped and terrified. A friend recommended he come see me.

I asked Howard to pretend I had deposited $2 million in his bank account and he now had all the money he needed. "What would your life look like?" I asked him. "I would still have my business and my family, but my business would be very successful," he quickly replied.

"Well, here's your $2 million," I said playfully. "Tell me how you would use it to make your business successful."

He thought for a moment and then easily came up with ten ideas to get more business. Some of his ideas would take lots of money, others wouldn't. By going through the list, we were able to come up with five action steps that didn't cost anything. These included meeting with potential corporate clients and putting up a flier announcing a 4-week intensive foreign language course.

We discussed the power of taking action as well as his energy continuum. He outlined a personal five-step plan for getting his energy to the high-end each day before taking any action steps. He recognized that his depression had been making his circumstances worse. He had a major breakthrough in his outlook – from negative to positive.

I only saw Howard for one session. Two years later, he is still thanking me. That one session turned his life and business around. He says I gave him a fresh perspective on life that inspired him to make positive changes. Energy work and "taking action in spite of circumstances" made him very successful. His business is thriving today, and his marriage is happy.

Getting A Different View

Here are questions to ask yourself to get some fresh ideas or a new perspective on your career:

1. If I had $2 million in my bank account right now, how would I be feeling and what would I be doing differently?

2. When I'm old and ready to die, how will I reflect back on my work and the choices I've made in my career?

3. When my life is over, what will I be most proud of in my work?

"You cannot solve a problem with the same mind that created the problem."

Albert Einstein

Einstein believed in the power of new perspective. When our days are filled with deadlines, meetings, projects, traffic, family chores, and the many dramas that fill our lives, we lose perspective.

You've probably experienced the refreshing power of going for a long walk. Suddenly you find yourself breathing a little deeper, stretching your muscles, using your eyes to take in vast panoramas instead of confined spaces. After a little while, you find yourself reflecting on problems in your day-to-day life. Often, a new idea will pop into your head. It could be the "perfect" solution to a problem you've been tossing around.

The biggest problem facing someone who needs to make a career change is that they need to "let go of what they know." In other words, shake the limitations out of their thinking. Have you ever tossed and turned all night trying to solve a problem and suddenly realized that you're just rethinking the same thoughts over and over without any new perspectives?

Our minds have limited access to a larger perspective when we're caught in the trap of worry and anxiety – which is our negativity. That fear-based state of mind produces a reduction of ideas. We close down into survival mode; our fear prevents us from opening our minds to fresh possibilities.

When we're at the high-end of our energy continuum *(feeling optimism and inspiration)*, we see everything from an expansive viewpoint. New possibilities reveal themselves.

The value in this new perspective is tremendous. We need to break through the negative thinking that is preventing us from taking action in a positive direction.

Every life transition deserves a tremendous amount of attention and good energy to be successful. Simply noticing that we are in pain and need to make a change is not enough. Complaining about it is not enough. We need to tap into our positive energy, take action, and move forward. This happens when we get a new way of looking and thinking about life. And that only happens when we move from our negative state to our positive state.

Getting a New Life

It's very important to pull out of your daily drama in order to get clarity.

1. Take a **career workshop**.

2. Take a **spiritual retreat**.

3. Take a **backpacking trip** with an insightful friend who will share life dreams.

4. See a **therapist or career counselor** for five sessions; discover what you really long to do.

Letting Go of What You Know

1. Get out of town! (Take a trip to someplace you've never been before.)

2. Do something crazy. Get a new hairstyle. Wear a silly new outfit.

3. Try skydiving, rock climbing, river rafting or hang gliding.

4. Travel to another country.

5. Get outdoors. Go hiking or boating. At the very least, go for a long walk.

6. Read a book about the life of someone courageous – such as the Arctic explorer Shackleton.

7. Watch a ridiculous comedy and laugh until you cry.

Questions to ask before going in a new direction

1. If I were an animal, what would I be and why?

2. If I could change to be a different animal, what would I become and why?

3. If I wrote a book telling my life story, what would I name my book?

4. In the next phase of my life, I will be more like...
   (name someone you admire)

5. In the next phase of my life, I will love my work passionately in the way (name someone who loves their work) does.

6. The part of myself that I will improve in the next phase of my life is...

7. Here's one baby step I will take in this new happier direction.

8. In the future, when I explain this turning point in my life and how I navigated successfully to a happier life, I'll say...

9. This is what I can do today to make my life happier...

Fill 'er Up Tip #15: Use a guide (an outside objective observer) to help you move through the labyrinth of limitations your mind puts on looking for a better career.

"You gain strength, courage, and confidence by every experience in which you really stop to look fear in the face...You must do the thing you think you cannot do."   *Eleanor Roosevelt*

When researching career coaches or counselors, ask to hear their life stories. Ask what they believe in. If they have a "negative" focus – leave immediately. Find someone with a positive attitude to help you, or you're wasting your time and money.

A good teacher, therapist, or counselor will serve you well. Here are some ideas for finding a good career counselor:

To evaluate a career counselor, ask the following questions:

1. What is your approach to career counseling? Explain it.

2. How would you define a positive outcome for us working together?

3. Which experts in the field of career counseling do you most admire?

4. How long (how many sessions) do you estimate it will take before I see results?

5. What is your life story?

6. What is your life philosophy?

Questions your career coach should ask YOU:

1. Tell me about your favorite job. What did you like about it most?

2. What has been your most miserable job and what did you hate about it?

3. What do you most love doing at your current or most recent job?

4. What do you dislike the most about your current or most recent job?

5. What are you really bad at in your current or most recent job?

6. Of all the managers you've had in your life, who was the best and why?

7. Of all the managers you've had in your life, who was the worst and why?

8. If you could start your own business, what business would you start?

9. If someone were going to pay you to go to school and get a degree, what degree would you get?

10. When you think of a job you would love doing, but it seems impossible, what comes to mind?

11. What is stopping you right now from pursuing the work you would love doing?

12. What were you put on this earth to do?

11 Ways to Get Through the Labyrinth of Limitations

1. Find a friend or an objective outsider willing to role play with you.

   A. **Spend five minutes telling this person why you can't find a job you love and why you can't pursue your dream career.** Your friend has to listen quietly for five minutes.

B. At the end of five minutes, pretending to be you they tell you what you told them. Listen and watch closely and look for the ridiculous roadblocks in their thinking.

C. Argue with them. Take the opposite point of view and tell them why and how they **can** find a job they love, and how they **can** pursue their dream career.

2. Write **ten reasons why you can't pursue your dream career.** Turn this list into a comedy routine. Present it to someone in a humorous way, making them laugh at you and with you. Laugh at yourself as well.

3. Sleep outdoors under the stars. Imagine **ten stars have secrets to tell you** about how to live a happy life. Write them down.

4. Pick a movie star or successful person you admire. Pretend to be them before they became famous. State all the reasons why you can't pursue the path that eventually made them famous. For example, **Julia Roberts explains why she'll never be a successful actress** and shouldn't waste her time pursuing that dream. Bill Gates explains why he just needs to get a job any job and stop dreaming. Make it funny and laugh, laugh, laugh.

5. Read a book of **poetry by Rumi, David Whyte, or Robert Frost.** Write one poem about something you love doing.

6. Write a **short biography of your life and put in a happy ending** in which you find work you love.

7. **Videotape yourself explaining why you can't find work you love.** Watch it. Videotape yourself talking about a dream career that has transformed your life with joy. Watch it and compare it to the first.

8. Invite ten friends to lunch. **Ask each of them to describe your best assets and what work they could see you happily doing.** Go around the table listening to each friend talk. Take notes. You can't speak, argue or answer while they talk – only listen.

9. **Write your elevator speech**; this is the 30 second pitch you would give to someone important you meet in an elevator. It tells them exactly what your gifts are and what you do really well.

10. **Call ten people in the line of work you're dreaming about.** (Be sure to fill your energy tank first). Present this elevator speech to them. Tell them you're not looking for a job but would like to ask for their career advice. Before hanging up, ask them to give you a name of someone who could help you.

11. Get a friend to interview you about your talents, passions, gifts and dream career. **They must write an Ad describing you as a successful business person.** Paste it to your bathroom mirror and read it every morning.

Resumes: What and Why?

What is a resume? It's a sales pitch that makes you look interesting enough to get an interview. That's it! It doesn't need to contain your life story, every job you've ever had, or every hobby you've ever pursued.

It's a sales pitch that must sell you within 10 seconds. Its primary winning ingredient is USER-FRIENDLINESS.

Consider this: If you answer a job ad, your resume goes into a pile of perhaps 500 to 1000 resumes. An overworked, underpaid Human Resource director goes through this pile and scans each document for an average of ten seconds. In that amount of time, he or she decides if you meet the requirements listed for the job and if you're worth interviewing. The answer is most often "no."

Why? Her job is to eliminate candidates who don't meet the requirements. It's her job to say "no" more often than "yes."

The more information you give, the longer you go on about yourself, the easier it is for Human Resource directors to find something that disqualifies you from the search. You're too old, have had too many jobs, haven't worked in the right field, are changing career directions too often, etc. Those are good reasons to get eliminated from the pile of potential candidates.

Resumes must sell your expertise and unique talents in the top three inches of the document. Or your chances of being considered for an interview are greatly reduced. Make it easy for HR and pack your sales pitch at the top. In the following pages you'll find examples.

Job experiences come after "areas of expertise." What's most important is what you do well and have done well. Later you can explain where you've done it and for how long. Your education always goes at the bottom. Please skip the hobbies altogether.

You must have a job objective at the top of your resume, and it must reflect exactly what the ad says. It can't be generic. It has to be specifically targeted to the job you're applying for. That's why your resume must live on your computer; you can tweak the objective each time you send it out.

You also need an attention grabber. I've invented a little paragraph that I call your "special spin." This is either a quote written by you that says why you love this type of work and how good at it you are. Or it's a testimonial from someone else saying how terrific you are. It must ooze with creativity and positive energy.

Remember, positive energy is everything. Do not put one word of negativity on your resume. Nothing bad has ever happened to you in your career or life as far as the resume goes. You can leave gaps in your work history to be filled in during the interview.

When you're sitting in front of them, present the truth about those time gaps. If you're at the high-end of your energy continuum (feeling love, optimism and inspiration), it won't phase them a bit that you were fired from your last job. They'll already be impressed by your energy. When written in a resume, however, this information can prevent you from ever getting an interview.

Only list the past ten years of your job history. List more than that, and they'll eliminate you (unfairly) due to age. During the interview, fill them in on the past 40 years of your career. Remember, the sole purpose of the resume is to get face time.

My clients report very favorable responses from the "special spin" paragraph. Human Resource directors have said the quote was the only reason they got the interview.

If you've had very little work experience, it's more important than ever to create a resume that celebrates your unique talents and passions with "areas of expertise" and a "special spin."

Two sample resumes are shown on the following pages.

Leslie England

2268 Green Ave in Denver, CO 80012

Phone/Fax 203-789-1234
Cellular 720-123-4567
leng@earthlink.net

Objective

A position as **Event Planner** which applies my background and expertise in management, budget planning, marketing, speaker recruitment, and publishing.

"I love planning conferences. The excitement of getting the best people, the best place, and targeting the best attendees, is always exhilarating. Blending so many diverse elements into a successful event in which everyone benefits is a bit like being an alchemist – turning raw materials into pure gold."
Leslie England

Areas of Expertise

◆ Planned, directed, and coordinated more than 40 multi-day conferences for thousands of attendees.

◆ Planned and implemented 100s of smaller events, training seminars, workshops, luncheons, and receptions.

◆ Implemented 50% increase in conference attendance.

◆ Recruited numerous New York Times best-selling authors for conferences.

◆ Created 250 brochures and 16 newsletters.

Professional Experience

Conference Director

1997 to Present   *Expo 2000*   Denver, CO

Researched and acquired speakers, developed seminar program and curriculum, negotiated speaker contracts, arranged travel and hotel contracts, created web content, and conference database.

Regional Administrator, Corporate Director & Event Director

1995 to August 1997   *League International*   Denver, CO

Planned and executed events & conferences, managed projects, planned and managed budget, wrote annual reports, news releases, brochures, marketing materials and grants. Conducted fundraising campaigns, provided staff education and training, and developed curriculum.

Education

BA in Humanities 1981   *Denver University*   Graduated with honors

Mike Mooney

330 South Quince Avenue
Spokane, Washington 90883

405-916-3219
mjm@nwinfo.net

Objective

A position as **GOLF CLUB MANAGER** which will apply my background and experience in business development & management, customer services, and problem solving.

Professional Profile

Self-starter with more than 17 years as CEO & CFO for independent businesses. Extensive public contact and expertise with customer complaints, insurance claims, problem solving, company policy enforcement, and staff management. Also have a passion for the game of golf.

"Many of my clients walk-in to pay their policies so that we can chat. They sit and tell me their troubles and concerns, and I help find solutions for them."
Mike Mooney

Professional Experience

◆ CEO & CFO Insurance Agency, Spokane, Washington –1995 to the present

◆ Built independent agency from scratch to an annual 2 million in sales.

◆ Developed trust and rapport with insurance clients.

◆ Built community reputation based on integrity and complete attention to customers' needs and concerns.

◆ Enforced company policies.

◆ Trained and managed staff, implemented employee handbook and employee negotiations.

◆ Created and oversaw budgets and marketing plans.

◆ Developed annual business plans.

◆ Oversaw all accounting functions from payroll to IRS forms and financial statements.

Education

Bachelor of Arts in Business Administration; University of Colorado

Certificates in Retail Merchandising and Management; Colorado Community College

Cover Letters

Your cover letter needs to be rewritten for each job you apply to. It needs to be concise, to the point and stating that you meet the exact qualifications they're looking for. Remember: Positive energy only and user-friendly always!

Here's an example:

Brown Paper Products
12 57th St.
Denver, CO 90084

Dear Mr. Gray,

I was pleased to learn of your need for a sales manager. I believe the qualities you seek are well matched by my track record:

Your needs:	**My Qualifications:**
Sales experience:	10+ years of sales expertise
Executive management experience:	Managed sales territories with sales revenue of $15 million annually.
Effective communication skills:	Provided presentations of enterprise solutions, value proposition, explicit needs analysis and project assessment.
Successful track record:	Assumed management of a territory performing at 56% of quota; achieved 112% of quota in first six months.

I've enclosed a resume that details my experience. I'd love to meet with you.

Sincerely,

Steve Cowley
44 Ontario Street
Erie, CO 50078

The Pitch Letter

When you've targeted a company you'd like to work for, and they aren't hiring, send a pitch letter instead of a resume. A resume would get lost in the HR office. But a pitch letter is sent directly to the person in the company who would hire you. It's user-friendly and is meant to spark interest in meeting you. Follow it with a phone call, and if your energy is great, you may get invited to a ten-minute meeting. If you get face time, you may be remembered when a position opens up. Or they may be so impressed with your energy they create a position just for you. **Here's an example** of a pitch letter. Remember to always follow a pitch letter with a phone call.

Rick Jones
Sports Media
1401 Oak St.
Suite 200
Dallas, Texas 90502

Dear Rick,

While working as an event planner, I created more than 40 multi-day conferences for thousands of attendees and implemented hundreds of smaller events such as training seminars, workshops and luncheons.

During that time, my marketing strategies increased conference attendance by 50%.

I'm writing to you because you may be in need of someone with my experience and capabilities to help you manage conferences.

Here are some other things I have done:

◆ Recruited numerous New York Times best-selling authors for conferences.

◆ Negotiated nearly 200 facility (hotel/conference) contracts for events.

◆ Created 250 brochures & 16 newsletters.

◆ Gave motivational lectures as a featured speaker at more than 30 national conferences.

I have a *BA in Humanities* from Mesa State College and a *paralegal certificate* from Denver Paralegal Institute.

It would be my pleasure to meet with you to discuss further details of my experience.

Sincerely,

John Hitchcock

Network: What it means and how to do it.

Your connections with other people (and your good energy) open doors. If you're recommended for the job – you're miles ahead of the pack. How do you make those connections? By networking.

Networking means getting the word out to everyone you know and everyone you meet that you're looking for a job, and you're very good at such and such. Here's what it really means:

When you meet someone, your positive energy is more powerful than any words you say. That person will walk away hardly remembering your name. But they WILL remember your energy. They'll tell someone else they were very impressed by you based on the quality of your energy – not the words you said.

Before going to parties, meetings, lunches or anywhere you're likely to meet people, fill your energy fuel-tank first. This is the most effective action you can take to find your new career.

Here are some other networking tips:

1. Buy software to **make business cards** on your computer, or go to a copy shop and have inexpensive ones made. They need your name, contact info, and a title such as Internet Technology Specialist, which is the title of the job you're seeking. If you make them on your computer, put a good photo of yourself on the card. If you're starting a new business, put your company name and tagline on the card.

2. **Give these cards to everyone** you meet. Whenever you hand out a card, give your elevator pitch. But mostly – pump the positive energy to everyone. This will cause a chain reaction of connections that will pull you into the right place at the right time.

3. **Your elevator pitch** is your 30 second (well-rehearsed) speech about what you do best and what kind of work you're looking for. Pretend you get into an elevator with someone who runs a major corporation. You have to sell yourself before the elevator gets to their floor. Write this speech down and practice it in front of a mirror until it's second nature. Then pitch it to everyone from waiters to your Uncle Harry. When you run into someone important, you'll know exactly what to say.

4. **Attend everything.** Go to Chamber of Commerce meetings, University Alumni gatherings, parties, church gatherings, and presentations given by business owners. Hand your card to everyone, and give your elevator pitch to everyone who will listen. Be a beacon of positive energy wherever you go.

5. When someone tells you they'll mention your name to someone who is hiring, **get the name of the person they're going to talk to as well as their name**. Write both names in your contact list.

6. Less than one week after that interaction, **call the hiring manager** and say you're following up on a lead given by so and so. Ask if your acquaintance has called yet. If not, give your elevator pitch. Be concise and friendly. Don't pester. Get your message across. Tell the hiring person that you'll send your resume and call again next week. Do both. Be sure to mention your acquaintance's name in your cover letter.

7. **Electronically send your resume and a short email** explaining what you're looking for to everyone in your email address book. Ask them to forward it to anyone who might be able to help you.

Information Interviews

This technique has been used for many years, but it's still a great tool for getting through closed doors. Here's the gist of it: Find out who has a job like the one you're trying to get. Call that person and **explain that you're trying to get started in the field they're working in. Ask if you can spend ten minutes with them (in person or on the phone).**

For example: **"I'm not looking for a job. I'm trying to get information about how to get my career going in this field, and you're the expert who could really help me. Could I please meet with you for just ten minutes to get some advice?"**

The trick here is to get the person talking about themselves. Ask very thoughtful questions about how they got started, what they love about the work, what they dislike about it, and what they recommend to someone who is just starting out.

You'll know you've done this well if they tell you their life story. Be passionately interested in what they have to say. Come away with at least one name of someone to call for more information. Keep making calls until someone says "So and so is hiring. I'll give your name to them."

When that happens, be sure to write down both names and do a follow-up call within a week. Send your resume with a cover letter mentioning the name of the person who suggested you speak to them.

Write your questions down before you pick up the phone. Here are a few to get you started:

Please tell me a bit about how you got started in this career...

What do you love about your job?

What's a good day at work like?

What is most challenging about your job?

What advice do you have for someone getting started in this field?

Is there anyone else you suggest I talk to?

The Magic Formula: Three Baby Steps

"Start by doing what's necessary, then what's possible, and suddenly you are doing the impossible."

Saint Francis of Assisi

Get Going

1. Write three baby steps you can take this week to make your dream happen.

2. Write three things you can do this week to feel better about yourself (such as exercise, eat healthy foods, etc.)

3. Write three things you can do this week to make your loved ones feel more loved and appreciated.

4. Write three things you can do this week to improve your life (like clean your room, sign up for a class, read an inspiring book, etc)

5. Do all of these things. Find someone who will look over what you've accomplished. It can be a friend or a coach or a counselor.

6. Keep going. Do three more of everything the next week.

7. Within four weeks, you will significantly improve your life.

"The road to happiness lies in two simple principles; find what it is that interests you and that you can do well, and when you find it put your whole soul into it — every bit of energy and ambition and natural ability you have."

John D. Rockefeller II

Write Your Life/Business Plan

1. Where do I REALLY want my life to be in one month?

2. Where do I REALLY want my life to be in six months?

3. One year from now?

4. Five years from now?

"A man can succeed at almost anything for which he has unlimited enthusiasm."

Charles Schwab

Russell's Story

Russell was an internet technology specialist at a mid-sized corporation. He had loved his work for more than 10 years, but now it was depressing him. He could barely go to work in the morning.

He knew he needed a change. When I asked what he really wanted, he said he had always wanted a Master's Degree in Divinity. He could see himself happily ministering to people in crisis and using his compassion and wisdom to help people.

He was intimidated by the thought of going back to school at his age. (He was in his 50s). He didn't want to give up a financially comfortable job to be a poor, struggling student.

We worked on changing his negative beliefs and thoughts about what was possible and what he deserved. We opened his mind to a new perspective. He focused on solutions and recognized how his fear was sabotaging his life. He took action steps to research his new dream.

Russell applied to graduate school, called the school director for an informational interview, and searched their college job board. His energy shifted dramatically to the high-end of his continuum. Within two months, he had a managerial position at the graduate school and was taking classes there. He felt like he had a new life and could live comfortably that way while he got his Master's Degree in Divinity.

Worrying about being a poor student had crippled him. He couldn't imagine how easily things would fall into place. When he moved to the high-end of his energy continuum and took action steps, doors opened.

"Imagination is more important than knowledge."
Albert Einstein

Get Inspired & Move Forward

When we're at the high end of our continuum, we're plugged into our inspiration. We're tapped into endless, boundless source energy which is where our brilliance originates. Work flows effortlessly, fluidly and exceeds expectations. When we're at the low end of our continuum, every task seems like overwhelming drudgery. Nothing is flowing and every chore takes twice as long as it should.

Before tackling the task of changing or launching your career – move your energy from drudgery to inspiration and tasks will flow effortlessly. Think of opening up to receive the work rather than forcing it. Know when to stop working and when to start working. That's the difference between inspiration and drudgery.

Everybody has their own unique way of moving from the drudgery state to inspiration or getting into the "groove." Think of matching your energy level to the task level. If it's a large and overwhelming task, you must be at the top of your fuel gauge before starting – so you'll have lots of fuel in your tank.

Write five steps you can do before starting a big task:

Examples: Go for a walk, laugh with a friend, see the project already finished, see yourself getting positive feedback for it, have a cup of tea, etc.

Write yours:

1.

2.

3.

4.

5.

Before you work on a resume, pitch letter or make a phone call, do the five steps you've written above. **Be aware of your energy level** before starting any project and that pile of paperwork on your desk will be taken care of effortlessly and with inspiration. You have NO excuses for not getting started. Just do it!

Chapter Seven

CHANGE IT!

Use the energy of change to move you forward.

To change is to be alive. Change is always the solution – not the problem. Our bodies are constantly changing; our cells replicating and dying. Our minds and spirits change as we have new experiences. Nature goes through never-ending cycles of death and rebirth.

When we're changing, we're in the flow of life. If we're not changing and moving forward, we're stagnant and cut off from source energy. From the high-end of our continuum, we can embrace change. We see it has always brought us to a better place, and we're unafraid (remember your fuel gauge).

Your career is not a solid, unchanging object. Your career is energy – just like everything else. It changes form as you interact with it. What works for you today, will change tomorrow. Five years from now, you may change directions again. That's a good thing! Learn to ride the wave of change, and your life will unfold naturally.

Write down an unexpected event that happened at least five years ago – that you were upset about at the time.

Write three good things that came from that experience.

Write down an approaching change and what scares you about it.

Write three good things that could possibly come from this change.

Write three current situations that really need to change but you've been afraid to initiate the change. Next to each one, write the first step you'd take to begin changing this situation.

Make a promise of three things you'll do to get happier. Write them down.

"When one door of happiness closes, another opens; but often we look so long at the closed door that we do not see the one which has been opened for us."

Helen Keller

> # YOUR TRUE WORK WILL CHANGE FORMS THROUGHOUT YOUR LIFE. PAY ATTENTION TO WHAT GOES ON INSIDE YOU AND AROUND YOU.

When I was in my 20s, I did numerous exercises to clarify my top values, needs and talents. Now, in my 50s, as I look back on what I wrote in my 20s, I am astounded at how drastically my values have changed over the years due to my life experiences.

In my 20s, adventure was my number one value. I taught mountaineering for Outward Bound School and was a serious rock climber. While I still enjoy a good adventure, my top value now is "helping others." Values guide us to our Brilliantwork. Our values change with every life experience we have. If our values remain the same, it means we're not living in the flow of life. Our energy is blocked.

Today we can turn on the television and watch world events dramatically unfolding. This new world perspective changes us day-by-day. You aren't the same person you were five years ago. The world is not the same place it was five years ago.

Remember the wild ride our economy took with the rise and fall of the Internet? Many people lost their jobs and reinvented their careers out of necessity. The tragedies of September 11, 2001 changed our values again. People wanted to find more meaning in their work after 9/11. I got a surge of new clients all searching for work that served the world.

"The best vision is insight."

Malcolm Forbes

I once worked for a visionary entrepreneur who taught me about the "constancy of change." He drew circles on the blackboard to demonstrate these cycles of change. He said that our lives moved from one circle to the next continually. At the top of a circle when things were going great, it was time to "jump" to a new circle (by making a huge change in direction). Or we could stay in the old circle/cycle and ride it down to the "crash" where we'd have to let go anyway. To have a successful life or business, you have to take the leap into a new direction when things are still going well, he explained.

When our ad sales were better than ever, our trade shows had record attendance, and our magazines were getting rave reviews, he would announce that we were going in a new direction with new products. He would "clean out the old energy" by laying people off and reinventing the business. It was all "energy" to him and he wanted to surround himself with "good energy people." He drove us crazy, and he was always right. He sold the company for millions of dollars just before the market crashed. Today he runs a thriving art gallery where he sells his extraordinary paintings for thousands of dollars. He has become a respected artist in his reinvented career – a huge shift in direction from entrepreneur and publisher.

"Not until we are lost do we begin to understand ourselves."

Henry David Thoreau

This brings me to a point that I'm often asked to address during seminars. "But I'm very successful at what I do. Shouldn't I just stick with it even if I'm bored?"

Beware of clinging to the past. Life will move on without you. Positive energy is free-flowing energy. Negative energy is stagnant. If you're stuck and not going anywhere, you're in the negative end of your continuum.

It's foolish to believe that things will never change. Things will ALWAYS change. Go with the flow. Jump in ahead of the wave and take the exhilarating ride. It's impossible to stand in the same spot anyway.

Once you become successful at something and feel like you're at the top of your game, go for a weekend retreat, or to see a career counselor. Get away from televisions, music, friends and family. Ask yourself what you value. Ask what you really want. Write three action steps you can take to explore a new direction.

What I Value Most
(or what is changing inside of me)

Five years ago, my top three values were: (example: independence, creativity, excitement, courage, helping others, security, adventure, financial gain, fame, honesty, integrity, success, stability, etc.)

Today, my top three values are:

What was most important to me five years ago?

What is most important to me today?

My dreams and hopes five years ago were:

My dreams and hopes today are:

Five years ago, I wanted to accomplish this:

Now, I hope to accomplish this:

The Five BrilliantWork Life Phases

Ask yourself which *BrilliantWork Life Phase* you are experiencing and how it is influencing your career direction:

The Tea Party   Imagine yourself at a tea party visiting with friends, having fun being social. The primary aspect of this life phase is being with other people, having fun with people, going to parties, feeling connected to a community of friends.

The Creative Tornado   Imagine finding yourself in the midst of a swirling tornado of creative energy. You feel driven to create something original, do creative work, leave your mark on the world, be artistic, funny, entertaining, dance, sing, or write. Life is still a lot of fun, but there is more end-result focus than the Tea Party phase.

The WorkHorse Phase   You've settled down and find yourself working very hard to accomplish things. You're working long hours, and sometimes feel exhausted. However you're good at your work and satisfied with the results. You're willing to keep at it for awhile. It's a very productive, successful time.

The Turning Point   Things you have always believed in are changing – all around you. You feel confused, unhappy with things you may have been happy with for many years. Suddenly, those things/jobs/roles feel very unsuited to you. You examine every aspect of yourself and reconsider your beliefs. At points it feels exciting, even sexy. At other times, it feels terrifying. You know you need to make a major change in direction.

The Wise Elder   Things are falling into place, and your life has meaning. You have embraced your new direction. You see a future of happiness and fulfillment. You feel peaceful, calm, deeply connected to the world and empathetic towards all people.

Write the name of the life phase you're experiencing and how it is affecting your career. Underline the phrases describing that life phase that most describe you right now.
Write down those phrases:

This is the life phase I'm experiencing and how it's affecting my career:

This is how I will make "change" my ally to move forward:

When you have a great job and suddenly lose it, it's a wake-up call. You've been sleeping and not paying attention to the changes going on inside of you and around you. Perhaps your soul was longing to leave that job long ago.

"What can any of us do with his talent but try to develop his vision, so that through frequent failures we may learn better what we have missed in the past."

William Carlos Williams

A Monday morning 9AM company meeting changed my life – not once but twice. I was VP of Content for a successful health website. We had been written about in *Time* and *Newsweek*, were meeting our sales goals, and had big plans for going public. I felt appreciated and that my work was helping people live healthy lives.

Rumors had been circulating that a big lay-off was coming because the market was changing and investors were losing interest in the Internet. By the end of the day, my job was gone and my stock shares were worthless. I was quickly offered a new job at an even better company – one that I had long admired. And it was closer to home.

I gratefully became VP of Content for the new company. Three months later, another Monday morning meeting – the company had been sold and I had lost my job, again.

When I reflect on that time, I see things very differently than I did when it was happening. I had worked successfully in the natural health industry for nearly 15 years and believed it was my niche and always would be.

Surprise! I wasn't enjoying it anymore and hadn't been since the birth of my daughter four years earlier. What happened to me? My values had changed when I became a mom. But I hadn't asked the important question: "What do I really want now?" I was afraid to rock the boat. I thought I could stay in one place indefinitely.

Remember, we are made of energy and always sending off vibrations. Everyone around us can feel our energy – even when we're denying it. I was sending off energetic messages that I was finished with this career and needed a change. Yet my words and actions were denying that truth.

The universal source felt my vibrations calling for a change and delivered it. I got exactly what I REALLY wanted. What do you really want right now? Chances are you're getting exactly that.

Top 4 Ways to Know if You're About to Lose Your Job

1. You're unhappy at work.

2. You don't like your boss.

3. You don't like your job.

4. You're dreaming of a new career.

Good Grief

If you're aware that a job is coming to an end, grieve for that job, let it go and move forward.

1. **Visualize yourself at your old (or current) office**. See yourself going through the day, doing your tasks.

2. **Imagine saying goodbye to everyone** and packing up your office. Put everything in a box and carry it out the door.

3. Turn around and look back at the building. Say, "I release this career path, **I release my identity around this job**, I release these people."

4. How do you feel? If there's sadness and grief in your heart, let yourself cry about it. Give the pain to God or to source energy.

5. Ask, **"What do I really want now?"**

Write your thoughts about releasing your old job or career path.

What would help you let it go?

How and when can you take that step?

Write down your plan to let go and move on.

"When you have decided what you believe, what you feel must be done, have the courage to stand alone and be counted."

Eleanor Roosevelt

I remember a great lesson I learned in my early 20s. I had been a shy schoolteacher. When my boyfriend of five years broke up with me, I decided I needed an adventure that would help me gain self-confidence. I signed up for a three-week Outward Bound survival course off the coast of Maine.

For three weeks, our group of 12 adults rowed through the foggy nights on a 20-foot open wooden pulling boat, slept on the open boat in the cold Maine nights, got seasick in the high swells of the summer storms, and survived three days and nights alone on a rainy island without food or shelter. I had never been so afraid, cold, hungry, sick, and exhilarated. I found strength and courage I didn't know I had. I broke through my fears and limitations. I turned negative thinking into positive thinking. Even though I had never previously run more than a mile, I successfully ran a 13-mile race around Hurricane Island at the end of the course.

When I returned to my life in Missouri, I felt reborn. I was functioning from the high-end of my continuum. I couldn't wait to share my experience with friends. I took up running and rock climbing as my hobbies.

Some of my friends, however, were shaken by the changes they saw in me. It threatened them.

I realized then that our closest friends and family are sometimes threatened when we change. It disturbs their sense of order. They may not have given themselves permission to change and grow, so they have trouble giving others that permission.

When we push on the borders of our limitations, we will lose the friends who can't expand with us. We may have to walk away from their negativity. New friends will appear as long as we're operating from the high-end.

One of my clients told me that her dearest friend was angry with her for looking for a better job. Her friend said to her, "What's wrong with you? You have security. You have a good income. Who is really happy anyway?"

She wasn't happy. And she couldn't stand to see her friend reach for happiness because she couldn't give herself permission to do it. You have to break away from this kind of negative thinking to have a better life.

There are solutions: Don't share your process with friends who won't understand it. Have an answer such as: **"You're right. I have a great job and great security. I probably won't change. But if I do, it will only be for something better."**

If you're unemployed say: **"I'm sure I'll find a job very soon. Don't worry. I'm not turning down any offers. I'll let you know when I have something."**

Just those simple responses will save you a lot of trouble.

"Exuberance is beauty."

William Blake

The Power & Beauty of Reinventing Yourself

Spend a little time watching the Biography channel, and you'll understand the importance of re-invention. Every successful person from Madonna to Nicole Kidman to Julia Roberts reinvents themselves periodically. They're effectively using change as their ally to move forward. The stars who survive for the long haul are the ones who periodically disappear from the public eye for a private regrouping. They reappear with a new look, boyfriend, musical style, and career direction.

Notice how quiet these successful people are about this rebirth process. You don't hear Madonna announce to the press that she's dropping out to get some cosmetic surgery, do some yoga, and reevaluate her direction. Instead, she quietly disappears. When she reappears looking terrific, with a brilliant new album, the press hails her as brilliant and savvy.

Your reinvention is just as necessary. Do it quietly. Don't announce your plans to change your life. Just quietly change it. When your career/life isn't heading in the right direction, quietly re-think it (do this workbook!), get a new haircut, change your energy, and only discuss your process with a chosen few (counselor, coach, or true friend). When you reappear with your new direction intact, you've successfully reinvented yourself; your friends will hail you as brilliant and savvy. (You are!)

6 Ways to Reinvent Yourself

1. Do this BrilliantWork Career Workbook.

2. Get your energy to the high-end of your continuum in spite of circumstances.

3. Get a new hairstyle and outfit.

4. Exercise and get healthy.

5. Spend time with people who inspire you. Listen and learn.

6. Make some new friends who only see you as your new self.

Create Your Spin

1. Write down what you will tell friends about your job search or career change.

2. Rehearse it in front of a mirror.

3. Call a friend and have a casual conversation. Insert your career "spin" into the conversation and see how it comes across. If your friend responds "that sounds great...good for you, etc.", then you've created a successful marketing spin. Stick with it.

Write down your new "spin" and rehearse it.

I see myself emerging as newly reinvented within this amount of time:

This is what I'll look like and what my career will be:

> # WHEN WE'RE IN OUR 40S, 50S, AND 60S, IT GETS HARDER TO CHANGE. HOWEVER, THE REWARDS ARE GREATER.

"Vitality shows not only in the ability to persist, but in the ability to start over."

F. Scott Fitzgerald

I have a 60-year-old client who is an inspiration to me. He had been comfortable in his corporate job for a long time and had only five years until retirement. But he wasn't accomplishing what he wanted to accomplish with his life. He had bigger dreams. His numerous health problems were frustrating him and making him believe he was too old to try something new. When I asked what he really wanted, he said he wanted to be recognized as a top-notch executive coach.

He worked for a large outplacement company. He asked his managers if he could focus on executive coaching. They told him it wasn't possible given their corporate structure, so he launched his own business at the age of 60.

His children were grown, but he supported his wife who was

attending graduate school. They had a nice lifestyle that he didn't want to lose. We devised a business plan that brought in a base income as he built his new client base. And we steadfastly turned around his negative beliefs about aging.

Within one year, he was successful and happy at his new life. His numerous health problems also improved. His wife was pleased and supported his dream. He recently told me that he is living at the high-end of his continuum now – feeling more happiness and good energy than ever. He's passionate about doing this work for the rest of his life. "I never saw myself retiring to play golf all day," he says.

Consider the possibility that every age-related health concern comes from negative beliefs about aging. What do you believe will happen to you as you age? You get what you believe. Choose to believe that you can tap into unlimited source energy when you're at the high-end of your continuum. Intend to have good health and boundless energy as you age. Don't listen to the negative messages all around you about aging. Find work you love and will love doing as you age. See yourself waking up each morning inspired to go to work. Use your work as a way to find meaning in life. That higher purpose will pull you to the high-end of your continuum.

The Myth of Retirement

Ask yourself honestly if your sense of worth is tied up in your work. For most of us, the answer is yes. Ask yourself honestly how you would feel if you woke up day-after-day with no place to go and no real work to do.

Playing golf and tennis will be fun – but not for 15 years. Your work is essential to happiness – believe it or not. I've had many "trust-fund babies" come see me in their 50s. They're desperate to find meaning in life, and they want to find work that makes them feel good. By going through this BrilliantWork process you can identify that work. Ask yourself, "What do I really want?"

Older & Wiser

1. How can I share my greatest wisdom with the world through my work?

2. What new passion have I found as I've aged?

3. What is my dream for a great life in my 60s and 70s?

4. What is my ideal retirement plan?

12 Ways to Stay Happy & Healthy as You Age

1. Go for a walk every morning.

2. Eat less sugar and processed foods; eat more fresh vegatables and protein.

3. Find work you love.

4. Keep dreaming!

5. Believe you can be healthy and happy as you age.

6. Focus on solutions instead of problems.

7. Forgive everyone.

8. Make a new best friend.

9. Turn off the TV and turn on Mozart.

10. See live performances of music, theatre, opera and dance.

11. Read great books that inspire you.

12. Recognize your negative energy and change it!

The work I would most love doing as I grow older is:

Fill 'er Up Tip #16: Ask for guidance.

In this book you've learned how your energy affects your life. You've taken responsibility for your life and your happiness. You know how to change your energy and focus on solutions. You've turned around your negative thoughts and beliefs. You've recognized your natural talents and passions. You've recognized what you really want. You live mostly from the high-end of your continuum.

But there will still be painful events that happen to you. You will have challenging circumstances in spite of your positive energy. My husband, Paul, died when I was 30 in spite of all my positive efforts and beliefs. These are agreements we make before a lifetime, so we can learn what we need to learn.

Your work is to "rise to the occasion" by getting your energy to the high-end – in spite of circumstances. This will make everything turn out much better than it seems at first. But sometimes, you just can't seem to do that. What then?

Ask for guidance. It is always there for you. You can call on God, the divine beings, the angels, or the source energy to pull you into the light. Simply ask to be lifted into good energy and out of the darkness. Your request will ALWAYS be answered. You are truly never alone – you just think you are. If only you knew who is standing beside you – you would never be afraid.

Let's summarize what we've learned in this BrilliantWork program:

Am I truly happy right now?

Where am I on my energy continuum?

What do I really want?

What is my dream for a perfect life?

What three things can I do each day to get my energy in a more positive place?

These are my top 3 natural talents:

My dream career is:

This was my past favorite job, and this is why I loved it:

I'm turning around my negative thoughts about work with this positive intention:

My pain fuels me to go in this new career direction:

These are my top three values, and this new career idea is in harmony with them:

When I visualize a day in the life of a career, I get a "yes" response to these careers:

My new diet of the heart includes:

From reviewing my life story, I can see these things makes me unique:

I'm turning around my fear of failure with this positive belief:

I'm turning around my fear of success with this positive belief:

My new career reinvention spin that I'll tell friends and family is:

I see myself emerging as newly reinvented within this amount of time:

This is what I'll look like and what my career will be:

If I died tomorrow, I would be most proud of:

I'm turning around my limited beliefs about money with
this positive intention:

My greatest passions are:

They lead me to this career:

This will get me back into the groove of life:

This is how I plan to let go of my old career and move forward:

I need to improve this part of myself:

The greatest insight I've gained from doing the BrilliantWork
career program is this:

Inspired by this insight, I will take these 5 action steps in
a new direction:

After you've completed the following page, contact me at **sue@brilliantwork.com** and we'll set up a session to process this information and get you going in your new direction.

Fill 'Er Up Tips:

1. Refocus your thoughts.

2. Move your energy.

3. Ignore your belittler.

4. Go on a diet of the heart.

5. Use EPR.

6. Dream it big to raise your energy.

7. Find out what you really want by playing your life backwards from end to beginning.

8. Identify your natural talents.

9. Find your passions.

10. Marinate in happy memories of past favorite jobs.

11. Use your intention.

12. Take the leap!

13. Use your deepest pain as fuel to find your BrilliantWork.

14. See the future you really want and believe it is possible.

15. Use a coach/counselor to move you through the mind's limitations.

16. Ask for guidance.

About  Sue Frederick

*As a rock climber and mountaineering instructor, Sue Frederick honed her teaching, mentoring and coaching skills while **leading extreme survival courses** through the Colorado Rocky Mountains for **Outward Bound**.*

*As a former **Vice President of Content** for Healthshop.com and Delicious Magazine she mastered the intricacies of corporate survival by being an authority on inspiration, and possessing a rare combination of emotional and spiritual intelligence. Today, as the **founder of BrilliantWork**, Sue is passionate about helping people and inspires them to bring joy and brilliance to their everyday lives. She was trained as a career counselor at the **University of Missouri** and is now on the **faculties of Naropa University** and **University of Colorado** where she teaches a course entitled "Finding Work You Love," as well as, "BrilliantDay: 7 Steps to Turn Your Day Around" from her book of the same name.*

*As a **student of spirituality**, Sue began studying Theosophy, yoga and meditation in the early '70s. She has meditated everyday for nearly 30 years and studied A Course in Miracles since the early '80s. Today she is a student of Swami Shambhavananda and the late Swami Muktananda, and she employs these seven steps successfully everyday in her business and as the mother of an eleven-year-old daughter.*

The *Continuum Series* of Books
from Frederick Malowany Publishing

BrilliantDay
7 Quick Solutions to Turn Your Day Around

BrilliantWork
7 Steps to Corporate Mastery

BrilliantLove
10 Steps to a Brilliant Relationship

All FM books are also available through
BrilliantWork™ at **www.brilliantwork.com**
or by phone: 303-939-8574.

Retail / Group discounts available.

BRILLIANTWORK
Putting personal and business power to work...brilliantly.

If you liked *Dancing At Your Desk*, **you will also like:**

7 Quick Solutions
to Turn Your Day Around

BRILLIANTDAY

Sue Frederick & Gene Malowany

"A brilliantly executed
Gift Book"

Who would *love* to own BrilliantDay?

Anyone who is...

→ going through a life transition

→ suffering grief from loss

→ needing a new way to look at old challenges

→ looking for better ways to inspire their team

→ longing for more positive energy in the workplace

→ searching for new and better solutions

→ trying to break old patterns

BrilliantDay eloquently guides you through 7 simple steps that lend a new perspective, help you make positive changes and get through painful or old challenges.

All FM books are also available through BrilliantWork™ at **www.brilliantwork.com** or by phone at 303-939-8574.

Retail / Group discounts available.

BRILLIANTWORK

Putting personal and business power to work...brilliantly.

Individual Career Counseling Sessions

Unlock your potential

There are secrets to finding and getting a great job and one-on-one BrilliantWork career counseling sessions will help you unlock them. Conducted **in person or by phone**, these individual sessions and "homework" provide a **concentrated format of assessment, evaluation and action** to help you move ahead quickly and confidently.

You'll be guided through a process that **helps you clarify your vision** of yourself, your work, your life:

Are you simply unhappy with your current job, or is it your career choice?
What values do you hold?
What changes do you really need?
What do you want, not only from work, but in your life?
And how do these things go together?

In evaluation, you'll take a closer look at what's in your way, what assets and talents you can take advantage of, your strengths, your weaknesses, how they affect each other and what you can and cannot control. From there, we'll help you take action by setting goals and creating a series of steps to take toward achieving them.

This is the BrilliantWork way to achieve joy in your life and passion in your work.

Get Started

Each individual career counseling **session lasts one hour** (by phone or in-person). **Choose one of the Programs** on the following page that you think may work best for you. You can always add sessions if you like. And if you're not sure, you can try a single session to help you evaluate your need.

Jump In

Single one-hour session

- Personal evaluation, assessment, guidance
- Homework and worksheets

Set Your Course

3 one-hour sessions

- Personal in-depth evaluation, assessment, guidance
- Homework and worksheets
- Value and skill clarification
- Interview preparation
- Job search strategy

Navigate Your Career

5 one-hour sessions

- Personal in-depth evaluation, assessment, guidance
- Homework and worksheets
- Value and skill clarification
- Interview preparation
- Job search strategy
- Professional resume creation
- Cover letter preparation

For more information, go to **www.brilliantwork.com** or contact **sue@brilliantwork.com** to get started.

BRILLIANTWORK

Putting personal and business power to work...brilliantly.

Hire a Speaker for Your Event

Sue Frederick's **inspiring keynotes, workshops and seminars** have delighted clients such as *First National Bank, National Association of Collegiate Career Counselors, New Hope Natural Media, Naropa University, Natural Products EXPO, eWomen Network and the University of Colorado.*

Her topics include:

Extreme Energy Makeover

Extreme Career Makeover

Dancing at Your Desk

7 Steps to Corporate Mastery

Loving the Work You Have

Finding Work You Love

Sue also offers **corporate consultations, executive coaching** and individual career counseling sessions (by phone or in person). Her work with corporations / executives has been described as *"A breath of fresh air"* and *"An enlightened new perspective on old topics."*

What other people are saying:

"People can't get enough of Sue Frederick's motivating presentations. Through creative thinking, humor, and excitement, people are inspired to take action in their lives. Sue is a rare find; a blend of truth, energy and knowledge that's hard to beat."
Laney Wax, *Curriculum Director*, **Naropa University**

"Sue exudes energy, passion and wisdom in her presentations. She is so engaged and engaging that she brings others to a point of taking action for positive change."
Lynne Brenner, *HR Director*, **New Hope Natural Media**

For more information, go to **www.brilliantwork.com** or contact **sue@brilliantwork.com** to get started.

7 Steps to Corporate Mastery Seminars

Making excellence the rule at your workplace

Sue Frederick's proven *7 Steps to Corporate Mastery Seminar* will transform your workplace. Using principles and examples fine-tuned over the years, this seminar teaches employees to:

- ▸▸ Define, set and focus on specific goals
- ▸▸ Encourage and reward innovative ideas and actions
- ▸▸ Motivate and manage with joy and inspiration
- ▸▸ Increase productivity and positive energy
- ▸▸ Embrace challenges
- ▸▸ Focus on solutions
- ▸▸ Identify innate talents
- ▸▸ Use change to their advantage

Make the most of your time

Sue Frederick's corporate **programs can be tailored** to business leaders, managers and staff, as well as, organizational time constraints.

There are a **variety of formats available**, ranging from one-hour seminars to intensive six-week courses, making it easy for you to "fit" BrilliantWork into even the most demanding schedules. Even better, this seminar will pay you back with multiple positive benefits for years to come.

For more information, go to **www.brilliantwork.com** or contact **sue@brilliantwork.com** to get started.

BRILLIANTWORK

Putting personal and business power to work...brilliantly.

"To be of service gives meaning
to life. In my work with clients
and in my keynotes, classes
and seminars, my goal is to help
people look at their lives in
new ways and find enlightened
solutions to their problems.
By increasing one person's joy
and success, we increase joy and
success for everyone."

Sue Frederick